MASTERING ML SYSTEM DESIGN INTERVIEWS

The definitive guide to AI-powered machine learning, AutoML, Edge Computing and federated learning

JORDAN RANUL & TOM TATE

© 2024 Jordan Ranul & Tom Tate All rights reserved.

The contents of this book may not be reproduced, duplicated, or transmitted without the written permission of the author or publisher.

Under no circumstances shall the publisher or author be held liable for any damages, compensation, or monetary loss due to the information contained in this book. Either directly or indirectly.

Legal Notice:

This book is protected by copyright. This book is intended for personal use only. You may not modify, distribute, sell, use, quote, or paraphrase any part or content of this book without the consent of the author or publisher.

Disclaimer Notice:

The information contained in this document has been provided for educational and entertainment purposes only. Every effort has been made to present accurate, current, reliable, and complete information. No warranties of any kind are intended or implied. Readers acknowledge that the author makes no commitment to provide legal, financial, medical, or professional advice. The contents of this book were derived from various sources. It is recommended that a licensed professional be consulted before trying the techniques described in this book.

By reading this document, the reader agrees that under no circumstances is the author liable for any losses, direct or indirect, incurred as a result of the use of the information contained in this document, including, but not limited to, - errors, omissions, or inaccuracies

Table of Contents

INTRODUCTION 7
Why ML System Design Interviews Matter 7
How to Use This Book 8
What's New 9

CHAPTER 1
UNDERSTANDING THE ML INTERVIEWING LANDSCAPE 11
The Current State of ML Hiring 11
Industry Demand 11
Key Trends and Industry Insights 12
What Interviewers Are Looking For 13
Preparing for Different Types of ML Interviews 14
Common Pitfalls and How to Avoid Them 15

CHAPTER 2
THE 6-STEP APPROACH TO ML SYSTEM DESIGN 17
Introduction to the 6-Step Framework 17
Step 1: Understanding the Problem 17
Step 2: Data Collection and Preprocessing 19
Step 3: Model Selection and Training 21
Step 4: Model Evaluation and Validation 22
Step 5: Deployment and Monitoring 23
Step 6: Iteration and Improvement 24
Common Pitfalls and Best Practices 24

CHAPTER 3
FUNDAMENTAL CONCEPTS AND BEST PRACTICES 27
Data Preprocessing and Feature Engineering 27
Model Selection and Hyperparameter Tuning 30
Model Evaluation and Validation Metrics 32
Scalability and Performance Optimization 34
Ethics and Fairness in ML 36
Conclusion 37

CHAPTER 4
REAL-WORLD CASE STUDIES 39
Case study 1: Visual search system 39

Problem statement and requirements 39
Data collection and pre-processing... 39
Model Selection and Training.. 40
Deployment and Monitoring 41
Main Lessons and Lessons Learned 42
Case Study 2: Real-Time Content Recommendation Engine 43
Problem Statement and Requirements 43
Data Collection and Pre-Processing 43
Model Selection and Training.. 44
Deployment and Monitoring 45
Main Lessons and Lessons Learned 46
Case Study 3: Advanced Fraud Detection System 47
Problem Statement and Requirements 47
Data Collection and Pre-Processing 47
Model Selection and Training.. 48
Implementation and Monitoring... 49
Key Aspects and Lessons Learned 50
Case Study 4: Personalized Health Predictions 50
Problem Statement and Requirements 50
Data Collection and Pre-Processing 51
Model Selection and Training.. 52
Deployment and Monitoring 53
Main Lessons and Lessons Learned 54
Conclusion 54

CHAPTER 5
ADVANCED ML SYSTEMS AND AI TRENDS. 55
Edge AI and on-device machine learning 55
Automated Machine Learning (AutoML)... 56
Federated Learning Systems.. 58
Integration with Cloud Platforms 60
Conclusion 62

CHAPTER 6
PRACTICAL EXERCISES AND SOLUTIONS... 63
Designing a Social Media Monitoring System 63
Problem 63
Step-by-Step Solution.. 63
Building a Scalable Recommendation Engine for E-Commerce............................ 67
Problem 67
Step-by-Step Solution.. 67
Develop a Real-Time Anomaly Detection System 70
Problem Description.. 70
Step-by-Step Solution.. 70
Create a Predictive Maintenance System 73

Problem Description 73
Step-by-Step Solution 73
Conclusion 75

CHAPTER 7
INDUSTRY INSIGHTS AND EXPERT INTERVIEWS 77
Insights from Top ML Engineers 77
Interviews with Industry Leaders 77
Key Trends and Future Directions 78
Preparing for a Career in ML 79
Career Pathways and Opportunities 79
Continuous Learning and Skills Development 80
Effective Job Search Strategies 80
Networking and Building One's Professional Brand 81
Conclusion 82

CHAPTER 8
COMPREHENSIVE PREPARATION TOOLS 83
Quick Reference Sheets 83
Key ML Algorithms 83
Evaluation Metrics 84
Common Interview Questions and How to Address Them 85
Technical Questions 85
Behavioral Questions 86
Checklists for the Day of the Interview 87
Pre-Interview Preparation 87
During the Interview 87
Follow-Up After the Interview 88

CONCLUSION 89
Summary of key concepts 89
Encouragement for continuous learning and development 91
Final tips for success 91

APPENDIX 93
Glossary of Terms 93
Additional Resources and Recommended Readings 96
Index 98
Conclusion 100

BONUS
DETAILED DIAGRAMS AND VISUAL AIDS 101
Industry Trends in ML Hiring Diagram: ML Hiring Trends 101
Overview of the ML Interview Process 102
Key Skills and Knowledge for ML Interviews 104

Data preprocessing techniques...106
Methods of adjusting hyperparameters..110
Evaluation metrics explained..112
Scaling strategies and performance optimization...113
Ethical and equity frameworks..115
Case study diagrams..117
Architecture of the visual search system..117
Workflow for real-time content recommendation..118
Architecture of the Visual Search System...118
Workflow for Real-Time Content Recommendation..119
Designing an advanced fraud detection system...120
Diagrams of Advanced ML Systems...124
Implementation of Artificial Intelligence on Edges...124
AutoML Workflow..124
Implementation of AI on Edge Devices...125
AutoML Workflow..125
Practical Exercise Solutions Visuals:..126
Designing a Social Media Monitoring System...127

Introduction

Why ML System Design Interviews Matter

Machine learning (ML) has rapidly become one of the most influential fields in technology, transforming industries from healthcare to finance, and from retail to autonomous systems. As ML continues to revolutionize how we approach problem-solving and innovation, the demand for skilled ML professionals has never been higher. Companies are not just looking for candidates who can build models; they seek individuals who can design comprehensive, scalable, and robust ML systems. This is why ML system design interviews have become a critical component of the hiring process.

1. **Real-World Problem-Solving:** ML system design interviews test your ability to tackle real-world problems. They go beyond theoretical knowledge, evaluating your practical skills in creating solutions that can handle large-scale data, provide accurate predictions, and maintain performance under various conditions. These interviews assess how well you can apply ML principles to solve complex, real-world challenges.
2. **Scalability and Efficiency:** In today's data-driven world, scalability and efficiency are paramount. Designing an ML system is not just about achieving high accuracy; it's also about creating solutions that can scale efficiently as data grows and user demands increase. Companies need systems that can handle growing data volumes and user bases without compromising on performance. This requires a deep understanding of system architecture, data engineering, and model optimization.
3. **Integration with Existing Infrastructure:** A well-designed ML system must integrate seamlessly with a company's existing infrastructure. This involves understanding data pipelines, deployment strategies, and monitoring systems to ensure smooth operation. ML system design interviews evaluate your ability to design systems that can be effectively integrated and maintained within a larger technological ecosystem.
4. **Cross-Disciplinary Skills:** ML system design requires a blend of skills from machine learning, software engineering, data engineering, and sometimes even domain-specific knowledge. These interviews test your ability to bring all these skills together to create a coherent and effective solution. Your ability to communicate complex ideas clearly and work collaboratively with cross-functional teams is also crucial.
5. **Innovation and Adaptability:** The field of ML is constantly evolving, with new techniques, tools, and best practices emerging regularly. ML system design interviews often include questions about the latest trends and innovations. They assess your ability to stay current with advancements in the field and apply cutting-edge techniques to your designs. This adaptability is critical for success in a fast-paced and ever-changing industry.

By mastering ML system design interviews, you position yourself as a valuable candidate capable of contributing to critical projects and driving technological advancements within a company. This book is your guide to achieving that mastery, equipping you with the knowledge and strategies needed to excel.

How to Use This Book

This book is structured to provide a comprehensive, yet practical approach to mastering ML system design interviews. Here's how to make the most of it:

1. **Start with the Basics:** Begin with Chapter 1 to understand the current landscape of ML interviews. This chapter sets the context by highlighting what interviewers are looking for and the skills you need to succeed. It also provides an overview of the ML hiring landscape, including key trends and industry insights.
2. **Learn the Framework:** In Chapter 2, you will be introduced to our simplified 6-step approach to ML system design. This framework will be your blueprint for tackling any system design question, providing a structured methodology to follow. Each step is detailed with practical examples and common pitfalls to avoid.
3. **Dive into Core Concepts:** Chapter 3 covers essential concepts and best practices in ML system design. This includes data preprocessing, model evaluation, scalability, and security considerations. Understanding these fundamentals is crucial before attempting more complex designs.
4. **Study Real-World Case Studies:** Chapters 4 and 5 present detailed case studies and advanced ML systems. Each case study includes problem statements, step-by-step solutions, and diagrams to illustrate key points. These chapters will help you see how theoretical concepts are applied in real-world scenarios.
5. **Practice with Exercises:** Chapter 6 offers practical exercises designed to simulate real interview questions. These exercises will help you apply what you've learned and build confidence in your problem-solving abilities. Each exercise includes detailed solutions and explanations.
6. **Gain Industry Insights:** Chapter 7 provides insights from industry experts and discusses emerging trends in ML. This chapter will help you stay updated with the latest developments and understand what top engineers are focusing on. It includes interviews with leading professionals and their advice for aspiring ML engineers.
7. **Prepare with Tools:** Chapter 8 includes comprehensive preparation tools such as cheat sheets, common interview questions, and checklists. Use these resources to streamline your study process and ensure you're fully prepared for your interviews. The checklists cover everything from pre-interview preparation to post-interview follow-up.
8. **Review and Reflect:** The conclusion will recap key concepts and encourage continuous learning. The appendix offers additional resources and a glossary of terms for quick reference. This section is designed to provide you with ongoing support as you continue to develop your skills and advance your career.

By following this structured approach, you will develop a deep understanding of ML system design and be well-prepared to tackle any interview challenge. Remember, mastering these interviews is not just about memorizing solutions, but about understanding the principles and being able to apply them flexibly to new problems.

What's New

The field of machine learning is dynamic and ever-evolving. Several key trends and advancements are shaping the landscape of ML system design. Staying current with these trends is crucial for success in interviews and on the job. Here are some of the most significant developments to be aware of:

1. **Edge AI and On-Device Machine Learning:** One of the most exciting trends in ML is the rise of edge AI, where models are deployed directly on devices rather than relying solely on cloud-based systems. This shift enables real-time processing, reduces latency, and enhances privacy by keeping data on the device. Understanding the architectures and challenges of edge AI is becoming increasingly important.
2. **Automated Machine Learning (AutoML):** AutoML is revolutionizing the way models are built and optimized. Tools like Google AutoML and H2O.ai are making it easier for non-experts to create high-performing models. Familiarity with AutoML tools and their applications can give you a competitive edge in interviews.
3. **Federated Learning:** Federated learning allows training models across decentralized devices or servers holding local data samples, without exchanging them. This approach addresses data privacy concerns and is particularly relevant in industries like healthcare and finance. Knowledge of federated learning principles and implementations is becoming essential.
4. **Explainable AI and Model Interpretability:** As ML models are increasingly used in critical applications, there is a growing demand for explainability and transparency. Techniques for making models interpretable are evolving, and understanding these methods is crucial for building trust and meeting regulatory requirements.
5. **Ethics and Fairness in AI:** The ethical implications of AI are gaining significant attention. Ensuring fairness, reducing bias, and maintaining transparency are critical components of modern ML system design. Interviewers are increasingly focusing on these aspects, so it's important to be well-versed in ethical AI practices.
6. **Integration with Cloud Platforms:** Cloud platforms like AWS, Google Cloud, and Azure continue to play a vital role in ML system deployment. These platforms offer various tools and services that simplify model deployment, scalability, and monitoring. Keeping up with the latest cloud integration strategies can help you design more efficient and cost-effective systems.
7. **Advanced ML Techniques:** New ML techniques and algorithms are continually being developed. Staying updated with the latest research and understanding how to apply these advancements can set you apart from other candidates. This includes areas like reinforcement learning, unsupervised learning, and neural architecture search.
8. **Real-Time Data Processing:** The need for real-time data processing is increasing,

especially in applications like fraud detection, recommendation systems, and autonomous systems. Knowledge of real-time data processing frameworks and techniques is becoming more relevant.
9. **ML Operations (MLOps):** MLOps combines machine learning, DevOps, and data engineering to automate and streamline the ML lifecycle. Understanding MLOps practices and tools can help you design more robust and maintainable ML systems.

By staying abreast of these trends and incorporating them into your study and practice, you will be well-prepared to tackle the challenges of ML system design interviews. This book is designed to help you navigate these developments and equip you with the knowledge and skills needed to succeed.

Chapter 1
Understanding the ML Interviewing Landscape

The Current State of ML Hiring

Overview of the Job Market

The demand for machine learning (ML) professionals has skyrocketed in recent years, is no exception. Companies across various industries, including technology, healthcare, finance, and retail, are increasingly integrating ML into their operations. This surge in demand has created numerous opportunities for individuals skilled in ML, from entry-level positions to senior roles.

Key Statistics:

- **Job Openings:** According to recent reports, there are over 100,000 job openings for ML professionals in the US alone, with many more globally.
- **Growth Rate:** The job market for ML and AI roles is expected to grow by 30% annually over the next five years.
- **Salary Trends:** The average salary for an ML engineer in the US is around $140,000 per year, with senior positions earning upwards of $200,000.

Industry Demand

1. **Technology:**

- Major tech companies like Google, Amazon, Facebook, and Microsoft are constantly on the lookout for ML talent to drive their AI initiatives. These companies offer some of the most competitive salaries and benefits in the industry.
- Startups in the AI and ML space are also burgeoning, creating innovative solutions and contributing to the demand for skilled professionals.

2. **Healthcare:**

- ML is transforming healthcare through applications in diagnostics, personalized medicine, and predictive analytics. Hospitals, research institutions, and biotech companies are investing heavily in ML talent to advance their capabilities.

3. **Finance:**
- Financial institutions are leveraging ML for fraud detection, algorithmic trading, risk management, and customer service automation. Banks, insurance companies, and fintech startups are major employers of ML engineers and data scientists.

4. **Retail:**
- E-commerce giants like Amazon and Alibaba use ML for recommendation systems, inventory management, and customer service. Retailers are also using ML for demand forecasting and personalized marketing.

Key Trends and Industry Insights

1. **Edge AI:**
- Edge AI involves deploying ML models directly on devices such as smartphones, IoT devices, and autonomous vehicles. This reduces latency and enhances privacy by keeping data processing local. The market for edge AI is expected to grow significantly, driven by advancements in hardware and software.

2. **Automated Machine Learning (AutoML):**
- AutoML tools are democratizing ML by enabling non-experts to build models with minimal manual intervention. This trend is making ML more accessible and increasing the demand for professionals who can leverage these tools effectively.

3. **Federated Learning:**
- Federated learning allows models to be trained across decentralized devices holding local data samples, without exchanging them. This approach addresses data privacy concerns and is gaining traction in sectors like healthcare and finance.

4. **Explainable AI and Model Interpretability:**
- As ML models are used in critical applications, there is a growing demand for explainability. Techniques for making models interpretable are evolving, helping build trust and meet regulatory requirements.

5. **Ethics and Fairness in AI:**
- Ensuring fairness, reducing bias, and maintaining transparency are critical components of modern ML system design. Companies are prioritizing ethical AI practices to avoid biases that can lead to unfair outcomes.

6. **Real-Time Data Processing:**

- The need for real-time data processing is increasing, especially in applications like fraud detection, recommendation systems, and autonomous systems. Real-time data frameworks and techniques are becoming more relevant.

7. **Integration with Cloud Platforms:**

- Cloud platforms like AWS, Google Cloud, and Azure offer various tools and services that simplify model deployment, scalability, and monitoring. These platforms are integral to modern ML workflows.

8. **ML Operations (MLOps):**

- MLOps combines machine learning, DevOps, and data engineering to automate and streamline the ML lifecycle. Understanding MLOps practices and tools is crucial for designing robust and maintainable ML systems.

What Interviewers Are Looking For

1. **Technical Competence:**

- **Programming Skills:** Proficiency in programming languages such as Python, R, and C++. Familiarity with ML libraries and frameworks like TensorFlow, PyTorch, and scikit-learn.
- **Mathematical Foundation:** Strong understanding of statistics, linear algebra, calculus, and probability theory. These foundational skills are critical for developing and understanding ML algorithms.
- **ML Algorithms and Models:** Deep knowledge of various ML algorithms, including supervised and unsupervised learning, neural networks, and reinforcement learning. Understanding when and how to apply different algorithms is essential.

2. **Problem-Solving Ability:**

- **System Design:** Ability to design scalable and efficient ML systems from scratch. This includes understanding the end-to-end process of data collection, preprocessing, model training, evaluation, and deployment.
- **Analytical Thinking:** Skill in breaking down complex problems into manageable parts and applying appropriate ML techniques to solve them. Interviewers look for a structured approach to problem-solving.

3. **Practical Experience:**

- **Project Experience:** Demonstrated experience in working on ML projects, including hands-on experience with data manipulation, model building, and deployment. Real-world project experience is highly valued.
- **Industry Applications:** Familiarity with applying ML techniques in real-world scenarios and understanding industry-specific challenges. This shows the ability to translate theory into practice.

4. **Communication Skills:**

- **Technical Communication:** Ability to explain complex technical concepts clearly and concisely to both technical and non-technical audiences. Effective communication is crucial for collaboration and stakeholder engagement.
- **Collaboration:** Strong teamwork and collaboration skills, especially in a remote or hybrid work environment. Being able to work well with others and contribute to team success is essential.

5. **Soft Skills:**

- **Adaptability:** Willingness to learn and adapt to new technologies and methodologies. The field of ML is rapidly evolving, and adaptability is key to staying relevant.
- **Ethical Considerations:** Awareness of the ethical implications of ML and commitment to developing fair and transparent models. Ethical sensitivity is increasingly important in ML roles.

Preparing for Different Types of ML Interviews

1. **Technical Interviews:**

- **Coding Challenges:** Expect to solve coding problems related to data structures, algorithms, and basic programming tasks. Proficiency in languages like Python and knowledge of libraries like NumPy and pandas are essential.
- **Algorithm Design:** Be prepared to design and analyze algorithms, particularly those relevant to ML. Understanding time and space complexity is crucial.
- **ML Conceptual Questions:** Interviewers may ask about fundamental ML concepts such as supervised vs. unsupervised learning, bias-variance tradeoff, and evaluation metrics.

2. **System Design Interviews:**

- **End-to-End System Design:** You'll need to design an ML system from scratch, considering aspects like data collection, preprocessing, model training, evaluation, deployment, and monitoring.
- **Scalability and Performance:** Focus on designing systems that can scale efficiently and handle large datasets. Discuss techniques like distributed computing, parallel processing, and model optimization.
- **Integration and Maintenance:** Consider how the system integrates with existing infrastructure and how it will be maintained and updated over time.

3. **Behavioral Interviews:**

- **Teamwork and Collaboration:** Be ready to discuss past experiences working in teams, handling conflicts, and contributing to team success. Highlight examples where you collaborated with cross-functional teams.
- **Problem-Solving Approach:** Explain your approach to problem-solving, including

how you break down complex problems, prioritize tasks, and develop solutions. Use the STAR (Situation, Task, Action, Result) method to structure your responses.
- **Adaptability and Learning:** Showcase your ability to adapt to new challenges and learn new skills. Provide examples of how you have kept up with advancements in ML and applied new knowledge to your projects.

4. **Case Study Interviews:**

- **Real-World Problems:** You may be given a case study involving a real-world problem that requires an ML solution. Discuss your approach to understanding the problem, gathering data, selecting models, and evaluating results.
- **Hands-On Tasks:** Some interviews may include hands-on tasks where you need to implement a solution in real-time. Practice coding and implementing ML models in a time-constrained environment.
- **Business Impact:** Consider the business impact of your solutions. Discuss how your approach can improve key metrics, drive revenue, or enhance user experience.

Common Pitfalls and How to Avoid Them

1. **Lack of Preparation:**

- **Solution:** Thorough preparation is key. Use resources like this book, online courses, and practice problems to build your skills. Schedule regular study sessions and focus on areas where you need improvement.

2. **Inadequate Understanding of Fundamentals:**

- **Solution:** Ensure you have a strong grasp of ML fundamentals. Review key concepts, algorithms, and mathematical foundations regularly. Use flashcards, quizzes, and summaries to reinforce your knowledge.

3. **Poor Communication Skills:**

- **Solution:** Practice explaining complex technical concepts in simple terms. Join study groups or find a study partner to practice mock interviews. Record yourself explaining concepts and review the recordings to improve clarity and conciseness.

4. **Overlooking System Design:**

- **Solution:** Pay attention to system design aspects, even if you excel at coding and algorithms. Study design patterns, architecture principles, and scalability techniques. Use whiteboard exercises to practice system design questions.

5. **Ignoring Ethical Considerations:**

- **Solution:** Stay informed about ethical issues in AI and ML. Read about case studies where ethical considerations were critical and think about how you would address similar issues. Be prepared to discuss how you ensure fairness and transparency in your models.

6. **Stress and Time Management:**

- **Solution:** Manage stress by practicing mindfulness and relaxation techniques. During the interview, stay calm and focused. Practice time management by timing yourself during mock interviews and coding challenges.

7. **Lack of Real-World Experience:**

- **Solution:** Gain practical experience by working on real-world projects, contributing to open-source projects, or participating in competitions like Kaggle. Hands-on experience is invaluable for building confidence and demonstrating your skills to interviewers.

By understanding the current state of ML hiring, key industry trends, and what interviewers are looking for, you can tailor your preparation to meet the demands of the job market. This chapter has provided a comprehensive overview to help you navigate the landscape of ML interviews in 2024. The following chapters will delve deeper into specific topics, providing you with the knowledge and tools you need to succeed

Chapter 2
The 6-Step Approach to ML System Design

Introduction to the 6-Step Framework

Designing an effective machine learning (ML) system involves a structured approach that ensures all aspects of the process are thoroughly considered and executed. The 6-step framework provides a comprehensive methodology to guide you through the entire life-cycle of an ML project, from understanding the problem to deploying and continuously improving the model. Each step in this framework is critical to the success of the project and helps ensure that the resulting system is robust, scalable, and effective.

The 6-Step Framework:

1. Understanding the Problem
2. Data Collection and Preprocessing
3. Model Selection and Training
4. Model Evaluation and Validation
5. Deployment and Monitoring
6. Iteration and Improvement

By following this structured approach, you can systematically address the complexities involved in ML system design and increase the likelihood of delivering successful outcomes.

Step 1: Understanding the Problem

1.1 Defining the Problem

The first step in any ML project is to clearly define the problem you are trying to solve. This involves understanding the business or research objective and translating it into a precise problem statement that can be addressed using ML techniques. A well-defined problem statement helps guide the entire project and ensures that efforts are focused on achieving the desired outcome.

KEY CONSIDERATIONS:

- **Business Objectives:** Understand the broader business goals and how the ML solution will contribute to these objectives.
- **Problem Scope:** Clearly define the scope of the problem. What are the inputs and desired outputs? What constraints and assumptions are in place?
- **Success Metrics:** Identify the metrics that will be used to measure the success of the solution. These could include accuracy, precision, recall, F1 score, or other relevant metrics.

1.2 Gathering Requirements

Gathering detailed requirements is essential for understanding the problem fully. This involves working closely with stakeholders to capture their needs and expectations. The requirements should cover both technical aspects and business considerations.

KEY CONSIDERATIONS:

- **Stakeholder Engagement:** Identify all stakeholders and involve them in the requirements-gathering process. This ensures that all perspectives are considered and that the solution aligns with business needs.
- **Functional Requirements:** Document the functional requirements, such as the specific tasks the ML system needs to perform.
- **Non-Functional Requirements:** Consider non-functional requirements, such as performance, scalability, security, and compliance.

1.3 Exploring the Domain

Domain knowledge is crucial for understanding the nuances of the problem and identifying relevant features for the model. This involves researching the domain, understanding industry practices, and leveraging expertise from domain specialists.

KEY CONSIDERATIONS:

- **Domain Research:** Conduct thorough research on the domain to understand the context of the problem.
- **Expert Consultation:** Engage with domain experts to gain insights and validate assumptions.
- **Data Sources:** Identify potential data sources relevant to the domain and evaluate their quality and availability.

1.4 Defining the Project Plan

A detailed project plan outlines the tasks, timelines, and resources required for the project. It serves as a roadmap for the team and helps manage expectations and track progress.

KEY CONSIDERATIONS:

- **Project Phases:** Break down the project into phases, such as data collection, model development, evaluation, and deployment.
- **Milestones:** Define key milestones and deliverables for each phase.
- **Resource Allocation:** Identify the resources needed, including personnel, data, and computational resources.
- **Risk Management:** Identify potential risks and develop mitigation strategies.

Step 2: Data Collection and Preprocessing

2.1 Data Collection

Data is the foundation of any ML project. Collecting high-quality, relevant data is crucial for building accurate models. The data collection process involves identifying data sources, gathering data, and ensuring its quality and completeness.

KEY CONSIDERATIONS:

- **Data Sources:** Identify and evaluate data sources, such as databases, APIs, web scraping, and third-party providers.
- **Data Relevance:** Ensure that the data collected is relevant to the problem and aligns with the requirements.
- **Data Quantity:** Determine the amount of data needed. More data generally leads to better models, but quality is more important than quantity.
- **Data Quality:** Assess the quality of the data, including accuracy, completeness, and consistency.

2.2 Data Cleaning

Raw data often contains noise, missing values, and inconsistencies. Data cleaning involves processing the data to improve its quality and suitability for modeling.

KEY CONSIDERATIONS:

- **Handling Missing Data:** Identify missing values and decide how to handle them, whether through imputation, deletion, or other methods.
- **Removing Outliers:** Detect and remove outliers that could skew the model's performance.
- **Standardizing Formats:** Ensure consistency in data formats, such as dates and categorical variables.
- **Addressing Duplicates:** Identify and remove duplicate records to avoid bias in the model.

2.3 Data Transformation

Data transformation involves converting data into a suitable format for modeling. This includes scaling, normalization, encoding categorical variables, and creating new features.

KEY CONSIDERATIONS:

- **Scaling and Normalization:** Apply techniques like min-max scaling or z-score normalization to bring features to a similar scale.
- **Encoding Categorical Variables:** Convert categorical variables into numerical format using techniques like one-hot encoding or label encoding.
- **Feature Engineering:** Create new features from existing data to enhance model performance. This could involve domain-specific knowledge and creativity.
- **Dimensionality Reduction:** Reduce the number of features using techniques like Principal Component Analysis (PCA) to improve model efficiency.

2.4 Data Splitting

Splitting the data into training, validation, and test sets is crucial for evaluating model performance and preventing overfitting.

KEY CONSIDERATIONS:

- **Training Set:** Used to train the model. It should be representative of the overall dataset.
- **Validation Set:** Used to tune hyperparameters and select the best model. It helps in assessing the model's performance during development.
- **Test Set:** Used to evaluate the final model's performance on unseen data. It provides an unbiased estimate of the model's generalization ability.

Step 3: Model Selection and Training

3.1 Selecting the Right Model

Choosing the appropriate model is critical for achieving high performance. The selection depends on the problem type, data characteristics, and project requirements.

Key Considerations:

- **Problem Type:** Determine whether the problem is a classification, regression, clustering, or other type.
- **Model Complexity:** Balance between model complexity and interpretability. Complex models like deep neural networks may offer higher accuracy but are harder to interpret.
- **Algorithm Suitability:** Evaluate different algorithms for their suitability to the problem. Consider factors like data size, feature types, and computational resources.
- **Benchmarking:** Compare different models using cross-validation to identify the best performing one.

3.2 Model Training

Training the model involves feeding the data into the algorithm and allowing it to learn the patterns and relationships.

Key Considerations:

- **Training Process:** Understand the algorithm's training process and configure it accordingly. This may involve setting parameters like learning rate, batch size, and number of epochs.
- **Handling Overfitting:** Implement techniques to prevent overfitting, such as regularization, dropout, and early stopping.
- **Monitoring Training:** Track the training process using metrics like loss and accuracy. Use visualization tools to monitor progress and detect issues early.
- **Parallel and Distributed Training:** For large datasets and complex models, consider parallel and distributed training techniques to speed up the process.

Step 4: Model Evaluation and Validation

4.1 Evaluation Metrics

Choosing the right evaluation metrics is essential for assessing model performance. Different metrics provide different insights into the model's behavior.

KEY CONSIDERATIONS:

- **Classification Metrics:** Accuracy, precision, recall, F1 score, ROC-AUC, etc.
- **Regression Metrics:** Mean Squared Error (MSE), Root Mean Squared Error (RMSE), Mean Absolute Error (MAE), R-squared, etc.
- **Clustering Metrics:** Silhouette score, Davies-Bouldin index, etc.
- **Explainability:** Use explainability techniques like SHAP values or LIME to understand model predictions.

4.2 Cross-Validation

Cross-validation is a technique for evaluating model performance by dividing the data into multiple folds and training/testing the model on each fold.

KEY CONSIDERATIONS:

- **K-Fold Cross-Validation:** Divide the data into k folds and train/test the model k times, each time using a different fold as the test set.
- **Stratified Cross-Validation:** Ensure each fold is representative of the overall class distribution, especially important for imbalanced datasets.
- **Leave-One-Out Cross-Validation:** A special case of k-fold where k equals the number of data points. It provides a thorough evaluation but is computationally expensive.

4.3 Hyperparameter Tuning

Hyperparameter tuning involves optimizing the model's hyperparameters to achieve the best performance.

KEY CONSIDERATIONS:

- **Grid Search:** Exhaustively search over a specified parameter grid. It's simple but can be computationally expensive.
- **Random Search:** Randomly sample hyperparameters from the specified distributions. It's more efficient than grid search.

- **Bayesian Optimization:** Use probabilistic models to select the best hyperparameters based on past evaluations.
- **Automated Hyperparameter Tuning:** Tools like Optuna or Hyperopt can automate and optimize the hyperparameter tuning process.

Step 5: Deployment and Monitoring

5.1 Model Deployment

Deploying the model involves integrating it into the production environment where it can make predictions on new data.

Key Considerations:

- **Deployment Environment:** Choose the appropriate environment for deployment, such as cloud, on-premise, or edge devices.
- **API Integration:** Expose the model as an API to allow other systems to interact with it. Tools like Flask, FastAPI, or AWS Lambda can be used.
- **Containerization:** Use containerization tools like Docker to package the model and its dependencies, ensuring consistency across different environments.
- **Scalability:** Ensure the deployment infrastructure can handle the expected load and scale as needed.

5.2 Model Monitoring

Monitoring the model in production is crucial for ensuring its performance and reliability over time.

Key Considerations:

- **Performance Monitoring:** Track key metrics like latency, throughput, and error rates to ensure the model is performing as expected.
- **Drift Detection:** Monitor for data drift and model drift, where the input data or model performance changes over time. Implement alerts to detect and address these issues.
- **Logging and Reporting:** Implement logging and reporting mechanisms to capture model predictions, errors, and other relevant information.
- **Retraining and Updating:** Develop a strategy for retraining and updating the model as new data becomes available or performance degrades.

Step 6: Iteration and Improvement

6.1 Continuous Improvement

ML system design is an iterative process. Continuously improving the model based on feedback and new data is essential for maintaining its performance and relevance.

KEY CONSIDERATIONS:

- **Feedback Loops:** Establish feedback loops to gather input from users and stakeholders. Use this feedback to identify areas for improvement.
- **Model Retraining:** Regularly retrain the model with new data to ensure it remains accurate and relevant.
- **A/B Testing:** Conduct A/B tests to compare different models or versions of the model and determine the best-performing one.
- **Performance Tuning:** Continuously tune the model and its parameters to enhance performance.

6.2 Experimentation and Innovation

Innovation and experimentation are key to advancing ML capabilities. Encourage a culture of experimentation within the team to explore new ideas and approaches.

KEY CONSIDERATIONS:

- **Experimentation Framework:** Implement an experimentation framework that allows for testing and evaluating new ideas in a controlled environment.
- **Research and Development:** Stay updated with the latest research in ML and AI. Encourage the team to experiment with new algorithms, techniques, and tools.
- **Collaboration:** Foster collaboration within the team and with external partners to share knowledge and drive innovation.

Common Pitfalls and Best Practices

7.1 Common Pitfalls

1. **Overfitting:**
   - Overfitting occurs when the model learns the training data too well, including noise and outliers, resulting in poor generalization to new data.

- **Mitigation:** Use regularization techniques, cross-validation, and simpler models to prevent overfitting.

2. **Data Quality Issues:**

- Poor quality data can lead to inaccurate models and unreliable predictions.
- **Mitigation:** Invest time in data cleaning and preprocessing to ensure data quality. Use techniques like data augmentation to improve data diversity.

3. **Ignoring Model Explainability:**

- Lack of model explainability can lead to mistrust and difficulty in diagnosing issues.
- **Mitigation:** Use explainability techniques and tools to make the model's predictions interpretable and transparent.

4. **Inadequate Testing and Validation:**

- Insufficient testing and validation can result in models that perform well in development but fail in production.
- **Mitigation:** Implement rigorous testing and validation processes, including cross-validation and stress testing.

5. **Failure to Monitor and Maintain Models:**

- Without proper monitoring, models can degrade over time, leading to poor performance.
- **Mitigation:** Establish robust monitoring and maintenance practices to ensure the model remains performant and reliable.

7.2 Best Practices

1. **Adopt a Structured Approach:**

- Follow a structured approach like the 6-step framework to ensure all aspects of the ML project are thoroughly addressed.

2. **Collaborate and Communicate:**

- Foster collaboration and communication within the team and with stakeholders. Regularly share progress and gather feedback.

3. **Invest in Data Quality:**

- Prioritize data quality and invest time in data cleaning and preprocessing. High-quality data is the foundation of successful ML models.

4. **Focus on Explainability:**

- Ensure the model's predictions are explainable and transparent. Use explainability techniques to build trust and facilitate diagnosis.

5. **Implement Robust Monitoring:**

- Establish robust monitoring and maintenance practices to ensure the model's performance remains high in production.

6. **Encourage Continuous Learning:**

- Stay updated with the latest developments in ML and AI. Encourage the team to continuously learn and experiment with new ideas.

By following this 6-step approach and adhering to best practices, you can design robust and effective ML systems that deliver reliable and scalable solutions. The next chapters will delve deeper into specific aspects of ML system design, providing you with the knowledge and tools needed to excel in your ML projects.

Chapter 3
Fundamental Concepts and Best Practices

Data Preprocessing and Feature Engineering

Data preprocessing and feature engineering are critical steps in the machine learning pipeline. Proper preprocessing ensures that the data is clean, consistent, and ready for modeling, while feature engineering creates meaningful features that can improve model performance.

Handling Missing Data

Missing data is a common issue in datasets and can significantly affect the performance of machine learning models if not handled correctly.

1. **Identifying Missing Data:**

- **Types of Missing Data:** Understand the types of missing data—missing completely at random (MCAR), missing at random (MAR), and missing not at random (MNAR).
- **Detection Methods:** Use methods like visual inspection, summary statistics, and specific functions (e.g., isnull() in Python) to identify missing values.

2. **Strategies for Handling Missing Data:**

- **Removal:** Remove rows or columns with missing values if the percentage of missing data is low and it doesn't compromise the dataset's integrity.
- **Imputation:** Replace missing values with estimated values. Common techniques include mean, median, or mode imputation for numerical data, and the most frequent category for categorical data.
- **Advanced Imputation:** Use model-based imputation techniques such as K-nearest neighbors (KNN), regression imputation, or iterative imputation methods.
- **Handling MNAR:** For data missing not at random, consider using domain knowledge or creating a separate category for missing values.

3. **Practical Example:**

- **Implementation:** Demonstrate how to handle missing data using Python libraries such as Pandas and Scikit-Learn.

```python
import pandas as pd
from sklearn.impute import SimpleImputer
```

Load dataset

```python
data = pd.read_csv('data.csv')
```

Identify missing values

```python
print(data.isnull().sum())
```

Mean imputation for numerical data

```python
numerical_imputer = SimpleImputer(strategy='mean')
data['numerical_column'] = numerical_imputer.fit_
    transform(data[['numerical_column']])
```

Mode imputation for categorical data

```python
categorical_imputer = SimpleImputer(strategy='most_frequent')
data['categorical_column'] = categorical_imputer.fit_
    transform(data[['categorical_column']])
```

Feature Scaling and Normalization

Feature scaling and normalization are essential for algorithms that are sensitive to the scale of the data, such as gradient descent-based algorithms.

1. **Understanding the Importance:**

- **Impact on Algorithms:** Scaling helps algorithms converge faster and achieve better performance. It ensures that features contribute equally to the distance calculations and gradient updates.
- **Types of Scaling:** Differentiate between scaling methods—standardization (z-score normalization) and min-max scaling.

2. **Techniques for Scaling and Normalization:**

- **Standardization:** Transform data to have a mean of 0 and a standard deviation of 1.
- **Min-Max Scaling:** Transform data to a specific range, usually [0, 1].
- **Robust Scaling:** Use median and interquartile range for scaling, which is less sensitive to outliers.

3. **Practical Example:**

- **Implementation:** Demonstrate how to scale and normalize data using Scikit-Learn.

```python
from sklearn.preprocessing import StandardScaler, MinMaxScaler,
    RobustScaler
```

Standardization

```
scaler = StandardScaler()
data['scaled_column'] = scaler.fit_transform(data[['column']])
```

Min-Max Scaling

```
scaler = MinMaxScaler()
data['scaled_column'] = scaler.fit_transform(data[['column']])
```

Robust Scaling

```
scaler = RobustScaler()
data['scaled_column'] = scaler.fit_transform(data[['column']])
```

Encoding Categorical Variables

Many machine learning algorithms require numerical input, so categorical variables must be encoded appropriately.

1. **Types of Categorical Encoding:**

- **Label Encoding:** Assigns a unique integer to each category. Suitable for ordinal categories.
- **One-Hot Encoding:** Creates binary columns for each category. Suitable for nominal categories.
- **Target Encoding:** Replaces categories with the mean of the target variable. Useful for high-cardinality categorical variables.
- **Frequency Encoding:** Replaces categories with their frequency in the dataset.

2. **Practical Example:**

- **Implementation:** Demonstrate how to encode categorical variables using Scikit-Learn and Pandas.

```
from sklearn.preprocessing import LabelEncoder, OneHotEncoder
import pandas as pd
```

Label Encoding

```
label_encoder = LabelEncoder()
data['encoded_column'] = label_encoder.fit_transform(data['categorical_column'])
```

One-Hot Encoding

```
data = pd.get_dummies(data, columns=['categorical_column'])
```

Target Encoding

```
Assuming a target column 'target'
target_mean = data.groupby('categorical_column')['target'].mean()
data['encoded_column'] = data['categorical_column'].map(target_mean)
```

Model Selection and Hyperparameter Tuning

Choosing the right model and optimizing its hyperparameters are crucial steps for building effective machine learning systems.

Choosing the Right Model

Selecting an appropriate model depends on various factors such as the problem type, data characteristics, and specific requirements.

1. **Problem Type:**

- **Classification vs. Regression:** Identify whether the problem is classification (predicting categories) or regression (predicting continuous values).
- **Other Types:** Consider clustering, dimensionality reduction, anomaly detection, etc.

2. **Data Characteristics:**

- **Size of the Dataset:** Some algorithms handle large datasets better than others.
- **Feature Types:** Choose models that handle categorical, numerical, or mixed types effectively.
- **Sparsity:** Consider algorithms that work well with sparse data (e.g., text data).

3. **Model Complexity:**

- **Simple Models:** Linear regression, logistic regression, decision trees.
- **Complex Models:** Random forests, gradient boosting, support vector machines, neural networks.

4. **Interpretability vs. Accuracy:**

- **Interpretability:** Simple models are easier to interpret and explain.
- **Accuracy:** Complex models often provide higher accuracy but are harder to interpret.

5. **Practical Example:**

- **Implementation:** Demonstrate how to select a model using Scikit-Learn's

```
from sklearn.model_selection import GridSearchCV
from sklearn.ensemble import RandomForestClassifier
```

Define model and parameter grid

```
model = RandomForestClassifier()
param_grid = {
'n_estimators': [100, 200, 300],
'max_depth': [None, 10, 20, 30]
}
```

Perform grid search

```
grid_search = GridSearchCV(model, param_grid, cv=5)
grid_search.fit(X_train, y_train)
```

Best model

```
best_model = grid_search.best_estimator_
```

Hyperparameter Optimization Techniques

Hyperparameter tuning involves finding the best set of parameters for a model to maximize its performance.

1. **Grid Search:**

- **Exhaustive Search:** Test all possible combinations of hyperparameters.
- **Pros and Cons:** Simple to implement but computationally expensive.

2. **Random Search:**

- **Random Sampling:** Randomly sample hyperparameters from specified distributions.
- **Efficiency:** More efficient than grid search, especially for large parameter spaces.

3. **Bayesian Optimization:**

- **Probabilistic Model:** Use a probabilistic model to guide the search for optimal hyperparameters.
- **Efficiency:** More efficient and effective for complex and high-dimensional parameter spaces.

4. **Automated Hyperparameter Tuning:**

- **Libraries:** Use libraries like Optuna, Hyperopt, or Scikit-Optimize for automated tuning.
- **Practical Example:**
- **Implementation:** Demonstrate how to use Optuna for hyperparameter tuning.

```
import optuna
    from sklearn.ensemble import RandomForestClassifier
    from sklearn.model_selection import cross_val_score
    def objective(trial):
    n_estimators = trial.suggest_int('n_estimators', 100, 300)
```

```python
    max_depth = trial.suggest_int('max_depth', 10, 30)
    model = RandomForestClassifier(n_estimators=n_estimators, max_depth=max_depth)
    score = cross_val_score(model, X_train, y_train, cv=5).mean()
    return score

study = optuna.create_study(direction='maximize')
study.optimize(objective, n_trials=100)
best_params = study.best_params
```

Model Evaluation and Validation Metrics

Evaluating and validating a model's performance is crucial for understanding its effectiveness and ensuring it generalizes well to unseen data.

Accuracy, Precision, Recall, F1 Score

These metrics are commonly used to evaluate classification models.

1. **Accuracy:**
- **Definition:** The ratio of correctly predicted instances to the total instances.
- **Limitations:** Can be misleading in the case of imbalanced datasets.

2. **Precision:**
- **Definition:** The ratio of true positive predictions to the total positive predictions.
- **Importance:** Measures the model's ability to correctly identify positive instances.

3. **Recall:**
- **Definition:** The ratio of true positive predictions to the total actual positives.
- **Importance:** Measures the model's ability to capture all relevant positive instances.

4. **F1 Score:**
- **Definition:** The harmonic mean of precision and recall.
- **Importance:** Provides a balanced measure of precision and recall.

5. **Practical Example:**
- **Implementation:** Demonstrate how to calculate these metrics using Scikit-Learn.

```
from sklearn.metrics import accuracy_score, precision_score, recall_score, f1_score
```

Predictions

```python
y_pred = best_model.predict(X_test)
```

Calculate metrics

```python
accuracy = accuracy_score(y_test, y_pred)
precision = precision_score(y_test, y_pred)
recall = recall_score(y_test, y_pred)
f1 = f1_score(y_test, y_pred)
print(f"Accuracy: {accuracy}")
print(f"Precision: {precision}")
print(f"Recall: {recall}")
print(f"F1 Score: {f1}")
```

ROC-AUC and Confusion Matrix

ROC-AUC and confusion matrix provide deeper insights into a model's performance, especially for imbalanced datasets.

1. **ROC-AUC:**

- **Definition:** Area Under the Receiver Operating Characteristic Curve. It plots the true positive rate against the false positive rate at various threshold settings.
- **Importance:** Provides a comprehensive measure of a model's performance across all classification thresholds.

2. **Confusion Matrix:**

- **Definition:** A matrix showing the true positives, false positives, true negatives, and false negatives.
- **Importance:** Helps understand the model's performance in detail.

3. **Practical Example:**

- **Implementation:** Demonstrate how to plot ROC-AUC and confusion matrix using Scikit-Learn.

```python
from sklearn.metrics import roc_auc_score, confusion_matrix, roc_curve
import matplotlib.pyplot as plt
```

ROC-AUC

```python
roc_auc = roc_auc_score(y_test, y_pred)
print(f"ROC-AUC: {roc_auc}")
```

Plot ROC Curve

```python
fpr, tpr, _ = roc_curve(y_test, y_pred)
plt.plot(fpr, tpr, label=f'ROC Curve (area = {roc_auc:.2f})')
plt.xlabel('False Positive Rate')
plt.ylabel('True Positive Rate')
plt.title('ROC Curve')
plt.legend()
```

```python
plt.show()
```

Confusion Matrix

```python
conf_matrix = confusion_matrix(y_test, y_pred)
print(f"Confusion Matrix:\n{conf_matrix}")
```

Scalability and Performance Optimization

Building scalable and performant ML systems ensures that they can handle large volumes of data and serve predictions efficiently.

Distributed and Parallel Processing

Distributed and parallel processing techniques are essential for handling large datasets and complex models.

1. **Distributed Computing:**

- **Frameworks:** Use frameworks like Apache Spark and Dask for distributed data processing.
- **Benefits:** Enables processing of large datasets by distributing tasks across multiple nodes.

2. **Parallel Processing:**

- **Techniques:** Use parallel processing techniques to speed up model training and inference.
- **Benefits:** Reduces training time and improves resource utilization.

3. **Practical Example:**

- **Implementation:** Demonstrate how to use Apache Spark for distributed processing.

```python
from pyspark.sql import SparkSession
```

Initialize Spark session

```python
spark = SparkSession.builder.appName('MLExample').getOrCreate()
```

Load data

```python
df = spark.read.csv('data.csv', header=True, inferSchema=True)
```

Data processing using Spark

```python
df = df.select('feature1', 'feature2', 'label')
df.show()
```

Data Pipeline Optimization

Optimizing data pipelines ensures efficient data flow from ingestion to model training and deployment.

1. **Pipeline Components:**

- **Ingestion:** Efficiently ingest data from various sources.
- **Processing:** Apply transformations, scaling, and encoding in a streamlined manner.
- **Storage:** Use efficient storage solutions like databases, data lakes, and data warehouses.

2. **Automation:**

- **Tools:** Use tools like Apache Airflow for pipeline orchestration and automation.
- **Benefits:** Ensures consistency and reduces manual effort.

3. **Practical Example:**

- **Implementation:** Demonstrate how to create and automate a data pipeline using Apache Airflow.

```python
from airflow import DAG
from airflow.operators.python_operator import PythonOperator
from datetime import datetime
```

Define default arguments

```python
default_args = {
    'owner': 'airflow',
    'depends_on_past': False,
    'start_date': datetime(2024, 1, 1),
    'email_on_failure': False,
}
```

Define the DAG

```python
dag = DAG('data_pipeline', default_args=default_args, schedule_interval='@daily')
```

Define the task

```python
def ingest_data():
```

Data ingestion logic

```python
    pass
```

Create the task

```python
ingest_task = PythonOperator(
    task_id='ingest_data',
```

```python
    python_callable=ingest_data,
    dag=dag,
)
```

Set task dependencies

```
ingest_task
```

Ethics and Fairness in ML

Ensuring ethical practices and fairness in ML models is crucial for building trust and avoiding biases.

Identifying and Mitigating Biases

Biases in ML models can lead to unfair and discriminatory outcomes. Identifying and mitigating these biases is essential.

1. **Types of Biases:**

- **Sampling Bias:** Occurs when the training data is not representative of the population.
- **Label Bias:** Arises from biased labeling processes.
- **Algorithmic Bias:** Introduced by the model itself due to its assumptions and design.

2. **Mitigation Techniques:**

- **Data Augmentation:** Enhance the diversity of the training data to reduce sampling bias.
- **Fairness Constraints:** Incorporate fairness constraints in the model training process.
- **Bias Detection Tools:** Use tools like AI Fairness 360 and Fairlearn to detect and mitigate biases.

3. **Practical Example:**

- **Implementation:** Demonstrate how to use AI Fairness 360 to detect and mitigate biases.

```python
from aif360.datasets import StandardDataset
from aif360.algorithms.preprocessing import Reweighing
```

Load dataset

```python
dataset = StandardDataset(data, label_name='label', protected_
    attribute_names=['gender'])
```

Apply reweighing to mitigate bias

```
RW = Reweighing()
dataset_transformed = RW.fit_transform(dataset)
```

Ensuring Transparency and Explainability

Transparent and explainable models help build trust and facilitate understanding of model decisions.

1. **Explainability Techniques:**

- **SHAP Values:** Use SHAP values to explain individual predictions.
- **LIME:** Use LIME for local interpretable model-agnostic explanations.
- **Model-Specific Methods:** Use techniques specific to certain models, like feature importance in tree-based models.

2. **Transparency Practices:**

- **Model Documentation:** Document the model development process, assumptions, and limitations.
- **Stakeholder Communication:** Communicate model decisions and impacts clearly to stakeholders.

3. **Practical Example:**

- **Implementation:** Demonstrate how to use SHAP for model explainability.

```
import shap
```

Load model and data

```
model = best_model
explainer = shap.Explainer(model, X_train)
shap_values = explainer(X_test)
```

Plot SHAP values

```
shap.summary_plot(shap_values, X_test)
```

Conclusion

By mastering these fundamental concepts and best practices, you can build robust, scalable, and ethical ML systems. This chapter has provided a comprehensive overview of essential techniques in data preprocessing, feature engineering, model selection, hyperparameter tuning, evaluation metrics, scalability, and fairness in ML. The following chapters will delve deeper into advanced topics, providing you with the knowledge and tools needed to excel in your ML projects.

Chapter 4
Real-world case studies

Case study 1: Visual search system

Problem statement and requirements

Visual search systems allow users to search for items using images instead of text. The demand for visual search technology has grown, particularly in e-commerce, where customers want to find products by simply uploading photos. This case study analyzes the development of a visual search system for an e-commerce platform.

Problem Description: Develop a visual search system that allows users to upload pictures of products and receive a list of similar items available on the platform.

Requirements:

1. **Accuracy:** High accuracy in matching uploaded images with similar products.
2. **Scalability:** Ability to handle millions of product images and thousands of searches per minute.
3. **Response Time:** Fast search results to ensure a seamless user experience.
4. **Integration:** Seamless integration with existing e-commerce platform.
5. **Monitoring:** Continuous monitoring to ensure high performance and accuracy.

Data collection and pre-processing.

1. **Data sources:**

- Product images from the e-commerce platform.
- Metadata for each product, including category, brand, and price.

2. **Data collection:**

- Extract images and metadata from the platform database.
- Ensure that images are labeled accurately and consistently.

3. **Data pre-processing:**

- **Image resizing:** Standardize image sizes to ensure uniform input sizes.
- Normalization: Normalize pixel values to improve model performance.
- **Augmentation:** Apply data augmentation techniques such as rotation, scaling and flipping to increase the diversity of the dataset.
- **Metadata processing:** Encode categorical metadata using techniques such as one-hot encoding.

Example implementation:

```python
from PIL import Image

import numpy as np
import os

    def preprocess_image(image_path, target_size=(224, 224)):
    image = Image.open(image_path)
    image = image.resize(target_size)
    image_array = np.array(image) / 255.0 # Normalize pixel values
    return image_array
```

Example usage

```python
image_path = 'path/to/image.jpg'
preprocessed_image = preprocess_image(image_path)
```

Model Selection and Training

1. **Model Selection:**

- **Convolutional Neural Networks (CNNs):** Use CNNs like ResNet or Inception for feature extraction.
- **Similarity Metrics:** Use cosine similarity or Euclidean distance to compare image embeddings.

2. **Training the Model:**

- **Pre-trained Models:** Start with pre-trained models on ImageNet and fine-tune them on the e-commerce product images.
- **Loss Function:** Use triplet loss or contrastive loss to train the model for similarity learning.

Implementation Example:

```python
from tensorflow.keras.applications import ResNet50
from tensorflow.keras.layers import GlobalAveragePooling2D, Dense, Input
```

```python
from tensorflow.keras.models import Model
```

Load pre-trained ResNet50 model

```python
base_model = ResNet50(weights='imagenet', include_top=False, input_tensor=Input(shape=(224, 224, 3)))
```

Add custom layers for feature extraction

```python
x = base_model.output
x = GlobalAveragePooling2D()(x)
x = Dense(256, activation='relu')(x) # Feature embedding layer
model = Model(inputs=base_model.input, outputs=x)
```

Freeze base model layers

```python
for layer in base_model.layers:
    layer.trainable = False
```

Compile the model

```python
model.compile(optimizer='adam', loss='triplet_loss')
```

Train the model

```python
model.fit(train_data, epochs=10, validation_data=val_data)
```

Deployment and Monitoring

1. **Deployment:**

- **API Development:** Develop an API to serve the model and handle image uploads.
- **Infrastructure:** Deploy the model on cloud services like AWS or Google Cloud using containerization tools like Docker.

2. **Monitoring:**

- **Performance Metrics:** Track metrics such as response time, accuracy, and user engagement.
- **Logging:** Implement logging to capture errors and system health.

Implementation Example:

```python
from flask import Flask, request, jsonify

import numpy as np

from tensorflow.keras.models import load_model
app = Flask(__name__)
model = load_model('path/to/model.h5')
```

```python
@app.route('/predict', methods=['POST'])
def predict():
    file = request.files['image']
    image = preprocess_image(file)
    embedding = model.predict(np.expand_dims(image, axis=0))
```

Find similar items using the embedding

```python
    similar_items = find_similar_items(embedding)
    return jsonify(similar_items)
def find_similar_items(embedding):
```

Implement similarity search logic here

```python
    pass
if __name__ == '__main__':
    app.run(debug=True)
```

Main Lessons and Lessons Learned

1. **Data Quality is Critical:**
- High-quality, well-labeled data is essential for training accurate models.

2. **Scalability Challenges:**
- Ensuring the system can handle a large number of images and searches requires careful planning and optimization.

3. **Continuous Monitoring:**
- Regularly monitor the system to maintain performance and accuracy, especially as new products are added.

4. **User Feedback:**
- Incorporate user feedback to improve the system continually.

Case Study 2: Real-Time Content Recommendation Engine

Problem Statement and Requirements

A content recommendation engine helps users discover relevant content based on their preferences and behavior. This case study explores the development of a real-time content recommendation engine for a streaming platform.

Problem Statement: Develop a recommendation engine that delivers personalized content recommendations in real-time based on user behavior and preferences.

Requirements:

1. **Personalization:** High level of personalization to ensure relevance.
2. **Scalability:** Ability to handle millions of users and real-time updates.
3. **Response Time:** Fast recommendations to enhance user experience.
4. **Integration:** Seamless integration with the existing platform.
5. **Monitoring:** Continuous monitoring to ensure relevance and performance.

Data Collection and Pre-Processing

1. **Data Sources:**

- User interaction data (views, likes, shares).
- Content metadata (genre, actors, release date).

2. **Data Collection:**

- Collect data from user interactions and content metadata from the platform's database.
- Ensure data is labeled accurately and consistently.

3. **Data Pre-Processing:**

- **User Interaction Data:** Aggregate and preprocess interaction data to capture user behavior patterns.
- **Content Metadata:** Encode categorical metadata using techniques like one-hot encoding.
- **Feature Engineering:** Create features that capture user preferences and content characteristics.

Implementation Example:

```python
import pandas as pd
from sklearn.preprocessing import OneHotEncoder
```

Load data

```python
interaction_data = pd.read_csv('interaction_data.csv')
content_data = pd.read_csv('content_data.csv')
```

Preprocess interaction data

```python
interaction_data['timestamp'] = pd.to_datetime(interaction_data['timestamp'])
interaction_data = interaction_data.sort_values(by='timestamp')
```

Encode content metadata

```python
encoder = OneHotEncoder()
encoded_metadata = encoder.fit_transform(content_data[['genre', 'actors']])
content_data = pd.concat([content_data, pd.DataFrame(encoded_metadata)], axis=1)
```

Model Selection and Training

1. **Model Selection:**

- **Collaborative Filtering:** Use collaborative filtering techniques like matrix factorization for user-item interactions.
- **Content-Based Filtering:** Use content-based filtering to recommend items similar to those the user has interacted with.

2. **Training the Model:**

- **Hybrid Model:** Combine collaborative and content-based filtering for better recommendations.
- **Deep Learning Models:** Use neural networks to capture complex user-item interactions.

Implementation Example:

```python
from sklearn.model_selection import train_test_split
from tensorflow.keras.models import Model
from tensorflow.keras.layers import Input, Embedding, Flatten, Dot, Dense
```

Prepare data for collaborative filtering

```python
user_ids = interaction_data['user_id'].unique()
item_ids = interaction_data['item_id'].unique()
user_id_map = {id: index for index, id in enumerate(user_ids)}
item_id_map = {id: index for index, id in enumerate(item_ids)}
```

```python
interaction_data['user_id'] = interaction_data['user_id'].map(user_id_map)
interaction_data['item_id'] = interaction_data['item_id'].map(item_id_map)
train, test = train_test_split(interaction_data, test_size=0.2, random_state=42)
```

Build collaborative filtering model

```python
user_input = Input(shape=(1,))
item_input = Input(shape=(1,))
user_embedding = Embedding(input_dim=len(user_ids), output_dim=50)(user_input)
item_embedding = Embedding(input_dim=len(item_ids), output_dim=50)(item_input)
user_vec = Flatten()(user_embedding)
item_vec = Flatten()(item_embedding)
dot_product = Dot(axes=1)([user_vec, item_vec])
model = Model(inputs=[user_input, item_input], outputs=dot_product)
model.compile(optimizer='adam', loss='mse')
```

Train the model

```python
model.fit([train['user_id'], train['item_id']], train['rating'],
    epochs=10, validation_data=([test['user_id'], test['item_id']],
    test['rating']))
```

Deployment and Monitoring

1. **Deployment:**

- **API Development:** Develop an API to serve the recommendation model and handle user requests.
- **Infrastructure:** Deploy the model on cloud services using containerization tools.

2. **Monitoring:**

- **Performance Metrics:** Track metrics such as click-through rate (CTR), conversion rate, and user engagement.
- **Logging:** Implement logging to capture errors and system health.

Implementation Example:

```python
from flask import Flask, request, jsonify

import numpy as np

from tensorflow.keras.models import load_model
```

```python
app = Flask(__name__)
model = load_model('path/to/model.h5')
@app.route('/recommend', methods=['POST'])
def recommend():
    user_id = request.json['user_id']
```

Generate recommendations

```python
    recommendations = generate_recommendations(user_id)
    return jsonify(recommendations)
def generate_recommendations(user_id):
```

Implement recommendation logic here

```python
    pass
if __name__ == '__main__':
    app.run(debug=True)
```

Main Lessons and Lessons Learned

1. **Personalization is Key:**

- Personalized recommendations significantly enhance user engagement.

2. **Real-Time Processing:**

- Implementing real-time recommendations requires efficient data processing and model inference.

3. **Continuous Monitoring:**

- Regularly monitor the system to maintain relevance and performance, especially as user preferences evolve.

4. **User Feedback:**

- Incorporate user feedback to continually improve recommendation accuracy.

Case Study 3: Advanced Fraud Detection System

Problem Statement and Requirements

Fraud detection systems are essential for financial institutions to identify and prevent fraudulent activities. This case study explores the development of an advanced fraud detection system for a bank.

Problem Statement: Develop a fraud detection system that identifies fraudulent transactions in real-time, minimizing false positives and false negatives.

Requirements:

1. **Accuracy:** High accuracy in detecting fraudulent transactions.
2. **Real-Time Detection:** Ability to identify fraud in real-time.
3. **Scalability:** Handle millions of transactions daily.
4. **Integration:** Seamless integration with the bank's existing systems.
5. **Monitoring:** Continuous monitoring to ensure high performance and adapt to new fraud patterns.

Data Collection and Pre-Processing

1. **Data Sources:**

- Transaction data (amount, location, time, merchant).
- User data (account details, transaction history).

2. **Data Collection:**

- Collect transaction and user data from the bank's databases.
- Ensure data is labeled accurately, with transactions marked as fraudulent or legitimate.

3. **Data Pre-Processing:**

- **Feature Engineering:** Create features that capture patterns indicative of fraud (e.g., transaction frequency, amount deviations).
- **Normalization:** Normalize numerical features to improve model performance.
- **Encoding:** Encode categorical features using techniques like one-hot encoding.

Implementation Example:

```
import pandas as pd
from sklearn.preprocessing import StandardScaler, OneHotEncoder
```

Load data

```
transaction_data = pd.read_csv('transaction_data.csv')
user_data = pd.read_csv('user_data.csv')
```

Feature engineering

```
transaction_data['transaction_hour'] = pd.to_datetime(transaction_
    data['transaction_time']).dt.hour
```

Normalize numerical features

```
scaler = StandardScaler()
transaction_data['amount'] = scaler.fit_transform(transaction_
    data[['amount']])
```

Encode categorical features

```
encoder = OneHotEncoder()
encoded_features = encoder.fit_transform(transaction_
    data[['merchant', 'location']])
transaction_data = pd.concat([transaction_data,
    pd.DataFrame(encoded_features)], axis=1)
```

Model Selection and Training

1. **Model Selection:**

- **Anomaly Detection Models:** Use models like isolation forests and one-class SVMs for identifying anomalies.
- **Supervised Learning Models:** Use supervised models like logistic regression, random forests, and gradient boosting for binary classification.

2. **Training the Model:**

- **Imbalanced Data Handling:** Use techniques like SMOTE (Synthetic Minority Over-sampling Technique) to balance the dataset.
- **Ensemble Methods:** Combine multiple models to improve accuracy and robustness.

Implementation Example:

```
from imblearn.over_sampling import SMOTE
from sklearn.ensemble import RandomForestClassifier
from sklearn.model_selection import train_test_split
```

Handle imbalanced data

```
smote = SMOTE()
```

```python
X_resampled, y_resampled = smote.fit_resample(transaction_data.
    drop('fraud', axis=1), transaction_data['fraud'])
```

Train-test split

```python
X_train, X_test, y_train, y_test = train_test_split(X_resampled, y_
    resampled, test_size=0.2, random_state=42)
```

Train the model

```python
model = RandomForestClassifier()
model.fit(X_train, y_train)
```

Evaluate the model

```python
y_pred = model.predict(X_test)
accuracy = accuracy_score(y_test, y_pred)
print(f"Accuracy: {accuracy}")
```

Implementation and Monitoring

1. **Deployment:**

- **API Development:** Develop an API to serve the fraud detection model and handle transaction data in real-time.
- **Infrastructure:** Deploy the model on cloud services using containerization tools.

2. **Monitoring:**

- **Performance Metrics:** Track metrics such as true positive rate (TPR), false positive rate (FPR), and precision.
- **Logging:** Implement logging to capture errors, model predictions, and system health.

Implementation Example:

```python
from flask import Flask, request, jsonify

import numpy as np

from sklearn.externals import joblib
app = Flask(__name__)
model = joblib.load('path/to/model.pkl')
@app.route('/detect_fraud', methods=['POST'])
def detect_fraud():
    transaction = request.json['transaction']
```

Preprocess transaction data

```python
preprocessed_transaction = preprocess_transaction(transaction)
```

Predict fraud

```
fraud_prediction = model.predict([preprocessed_transaction])
return jsonify({'fraud': bool(fraud_prediction)})
def preprocess_transaction(transaction):
```

Implement preprocessing logic here

```
pass
if __name__ == '__main__':
app.run(debug=True)
```

Key Aspects and Lessons Learned

1. **Real-Time Processing:**
- Real-time fraud detection requires efficient data processing and model inference.

2. **Imbalanced Data Handling:**
- Techniques like SMOTE are essential for handling imbalanced datasets and improving model performance.

3. **Continuous Monitoring:**
- Regularly monitor the system to maintain high performance and adapt to new fraud patterns.

4. **User Feedback:**
- Incorporate user feedback to improve the system continually and reduce false positives and false negatives.

Case Study 4: Personalized Health Predictions

Problem Statement and Requirements

Personalized health prediction systems use data to provide tailored health insights and recommendations. This case study explores the development of a personalized health prediction system for a healthcare provider.

Problem Statement: Develop a health prediction system that provides personalized health insights and recommendations based on individual health data.

Requirements:

1. **Accuracy:** High accuracy in health predictions.
2. **Personalization:** Tailored recommendations based on individual health data.
3. **Scalability:** Handle large volumes of health data.
4. **Integration:** Seamless integration with the healthcare provider's systems.
5. **Monitoring:** Continuous monitoring to ensure high performance and adapt to new health trends.

Data Collection and Pre-Processing

1. **Data Sources:**

- Electronic Health Records (EHRs)
- Wearable device data (heart rate, activity levels)
- Patient-reported data (symptoms, lifestyle information)

2. **Data Collection:**

- Collect data from EHRs, wearable devices, and patient reports.
- Ensure data is labeled accurately and consistently.

3. **Data Pre-Processing:**

- **Data Integration:** Integrate data from multiple sources to create a comprehensive dataset.
- **Normalization:** Normalize numerical features to improve model performance.
- **Encoding:** Encode categorical features using techniques like one-hot encoding.

Implementation Example:

```python
import pandas as pd
    from sklearn.preprocessing import StandardScaler, OneHotEncoder
```

Load data

```python
ehr_data = pd.read_csv('ehr_data.csv')
wearable_data = pd.read_csv('wearable_data.csv')
patient_data = pd.read_csv('patient_data.csv')
```

Integrate data

```python
health_data = pd.merge(ehr_data, wearable_data, on='patient_id')
health_data = pd.merge(health_data, patient_data, on='patient_id')
```

Normalize numerical features

```
scaler = StandardScaler()
health_data[['heart_rate', 'activity_level']] = scaler.fit_
    transform(health_data[['heart_rate', 'activity_level']])
```

Encode categorical features

```
encoder = OneHotEncoder()
encoded_features = encoder.fit_transform(health_data[['symptoms']])
health_data = pd.concat([health_data, pd.DataFrame(encoded_
    features)], axis=1)
```

Model Selection and Training

1. **Model Selection:**

- **Regression Models:** Use regression models for continuous health predictions (e.g., blood pressure, glucose levels).
- **Classification Models:** Use classification models for predicting health outcomes (e.g., risk of disease).

2. **Training the Model:**

- **Feature Selection:** Select relevant features for the prediction task.
- **Hyperparameter Tuning:** Use techniques like grid search to optimize model hyperparameters.

Implementation Example:

```
from sklearn.model_selection import train_test_split, GridSearchCV
from sklearn.linear_model import LinearRegression
```

Prepare data for regression

```
X = health_data.drop('blood_pressure', axis=1)
y = health_data['blood_pressure']
```

Train-test split

```
X_train, X_test, y_train, y_test = train_test_split(X, y, test_
    size=0.2, random_state=42)
```

Train the model

```
model = LinearRegression()
model.fit(X_train, y_train)
```

Evaluate the model

```
y_pred = model.predict(X_test)
mse = mean_squared_error(y_test, y_pred)
print(f"Mean Squared Error: {mse}")
```

Deployment and Monitoring

1. **Deployment:**

- **API Development:** Develop an API to serve the health prediction model and handle patient data.
- **Infrastructure:** Deploy the model on cloud services using containerization tools.

2. **Monitoring:**

- **Performance Metrics:** Track metrics such as prediction accuracy and user engagement.
- **Logging:** Implement logging to capture errors, model predictions, and system health.

Implementation Example:

```
from flask import Flask, request, jsonify
import numpy as np

    from sklearn.externals import joblib
    app = Flask(__name__)
    model = joblib.load('path/to/model.pkl')
    @app.route('/predict_health', methods=['POST'])
    def predict_health():
    patient_data = request.json['patient_data']
```

Preprocess patient data

```
    preprocessed_data = preprocess_data(patient_data)
```

Predict health outcome

```
    health_prediction = model.predict([preprocessed_data])
    return jsonify({'prediction': health_prediction})
    def preprocess_data(patient_data):
```

Implement preprocessing logic here

```
    pass
    if __name__ == '__main__':
    app.run(debug=True)
```

Main Lessons and Lessons Learned

1. **Personalization is Crucial:**
- Personalized health predictions significantly improve patient engagement and outcomes.

2. **Data Integration Challenges:**
- Integrating data from multiple sources requires careful planning and preprocessing.

3. **Continuous Monitoring:**
- Regularly monitor the system to maintain high performance and adapt to new health trends.

4. **User Feedback:**
- Incorporate user feedback to continually improve prediction accuracy and relevance.

Conclusion

These case studies provide a comprehensive overview of how to apply machine learning techniques to solve real-world problems in various domains. By understanding the problem statements, data collection, model selection, training, deployment, and monitoring processes, you can develop robust and effective ML systems. The lessons learned from these case studies will help you navigate the complexities of ML projects and deliver successful outcomes.

Chapter 5
Advanced ML systems and AI trends.

Edge AI and on-device machine learning

Edge AI and on-device machine learning are transforming the way data is processed and analyzed, bringing computation closer to the place where data is generated. This shift enables real-time processing, reduces latency, and improves privacy by keeping data local.

Architectures and use cases

1. **Architectures:**

- **Hardware accelerators:** Using specialized hardware such as GPUs, TPUs, and AI-specific chips (e.g., NVIDIA Jetson, Google Coral) designed to efficiently perform ML computations on the edge.
- **Model optimization:** Techniques such as quantization, pruning, and knowledge distillation to reduce model size and computational requirements while maintaining performance.
- **Edge Computing frameworks:** Tools and platforms such as TensorFlow Lite, OpenVINO and Apache MXNet optimized for edge deployment.

2. **Use cases:**

- **Smart Devices:** Applications in smartphones, wearables, and home automation systems. For example, voice assistants (e.g., Google Assistant, Amazon Alexa) locally process voice commands for faster response times.
- **Industrial IoT:** Predictive maintenance and real-time monitoring in manufacturing plants, where sensors and edge devices analyze data locally to predict equipment failures.
- **Healthcare:** Portable medical devices that monitor patients' vitals and provide real-time alerts for critical conditions without the need for constant Internet connectivity.
- **Autonomous vehicles:** Real-time object detection and navigation in self-driving cars, where immediate decision making is critical for safety.

Implementation example:

```
import tensorflow as tf
```

Load pre-trained model

model = tf.keras.models.load_model('path/to/model.h5')

Convert model to TensorFlow Lite format

converter = tf.lite.TFLiteConverter.from_keras_model(model)

tflite_model = converter.convert()

Save the converted model

with open('model.tflite', 'wb') as f:

f.write(tflite_model)

Benefits and Challenges

1. **Benefits:**

- **Reduced Latency:** Processing data locally minimizes latency, providing faster responses which are critical for real-time applications.
- **Enhanced Privacy:** Keeping data on-device reduces the risk of data breaches and enhances user privacy, as sensitive information does not need to be transmitted to the cloud.
- **Bandwidth Efficiency:** Reduces the need for continuous data transmission to central servers, saving bandwidth and lowering operational costs.
- **Scalability:** Distributing computation across multiple edge devices can scale more effectively than relying solely on centralized cloud resources.

2. **Challenges:**

- **Resource Constraints:** Edge devices have limited computational power, memory, and storage compared to cloud servers, requiring efficient model optimization techniques.
- **Model Deployment and Updates:** Managing the deployment and updates of models across numerous devices can be complex and requires robust MLOps practices.
- **Security Risks:** While on-device processing enhances privacy, it also introduces new security vulnerabilities that need to be addressed, such as physical tampering and malware attacks.
- **Data Fragmentation:** Data is often spread across many devices, making it challenging to aggregate and analyze at scale.

Automated Machine Learning (AutoML)

Automated Machine Learning (AutoML) aims to make ML accessible to non-experts by automating the end-to-end process of applying machine learning to real-world problems.

AutoML covers data preprocessing, feature engineering, model selection, hyperparameter tuning, and model evaluation.

Tools and Techniques

1. **Tools:**

- **Google AutoML:** A suite of machine learning products that enable developers to build high-quality custom models with minimal effort.
- **H2O.ai:** Provides tools like H2O AutoML, Driverless AI that automate the machine learning workflow.
- **TPOT:** An open-source AutoML tool that uses genetic algorithms to optimize machine learning pipelines.
- **AutoKeras:** An open-source software library built on Keras, designed to make deep learning accessible to everyone through AutoML.

2. **Techniques:**

- **Hyperparameter Optimization:** Automated search strategies like grid search, random search, Bayesian optimization, and evolutionary algorithms to find the best hyperparameters.
- **Neural Architecture Search (NAS):** Techniques to automate the design of neural network architectures, optimizing layers, neurons, and connections.
- **Feature Engineering:** Automated feature selection, extraction, and transformation using techniques like recursive feature elimination and principal component analysis (PCA).
- **Pipeline Optimization:** End-to-end pipeline optimization to automate the entire machine learning workflow, from data preprocessing to model deployment.

Implementation Example:

```python
from tpot import TPOTClassifier
from sklearn.model_selection import train_test_split
from sklearn.datasets import load_iris
```

Load data

```python
data = load_iris()
X_train, X_test, y_train, y_test = train_test_split(data.data, data.
    target, test_size=0.2, random_state=42)
```

Initialize and train TPOT classifier

```python
tpot = TPOTClassifier(verbosity=2, generations=5, population_size=20)
tpot.fit(X_train, y_train)
```

Evaluate the model

```python
print(tpot.score(X_test, y_test))
```

Export the best model pipeline

```
tpot.export('best_pipeline.py')
```

Applications and Best Practices

1. **Applications:**

- **Healthcare:** AutoML is used to develop models for disease prediction, medical imaging analysis, and personalized treatment recommendations.
- **Finance:** Used for credit scoring, fraud detection, and algorithmic trading, where rapid prototyping and deployment of models are essential.
- **Retail:** Applications in demand forecasting, customer segmentation, and personalized marketing.
- **Manufacturing:** Predictive maintenance, quality control, and supply chain optimization.

2. **Best Practices:**

- **Data Quality:** Ensure high-quality data input, as AutoML systems can only perform as well as the data they are provided.
- **Model Interpretability:** While AutoML can create complex models, it's crucial to use interpretability tools to understand and explain model predictions.
- **Domain Expertise:** Combine AutoML with domain expertise to guide the feature engineering process and interpret results effectively.
- **Iterative Refinement:** Use AutoML for initial model building and then iteratively refine the models with domain-specific tweaks and improvements.

Federated Learning Systems

Federated learning is a decentralized approach to training machine learning models where data remains on the local devices, and only model updates are shared. This approach addresses privacy concerns and allows for the utilization of data from various sources without centralizing it.

Principles and Implementation

1. **Principles:**

- **Decentralized Training:** Train models locally on devices and aggregate model updates centrally without sharing raw data.
- **Privacy Preservation:** Enhances privacy by keeping data localized, reducing the risk of data breaches.
- **Scalability:** Can leverage the computational power of numerous devices for training large-scale models.

2. Implementation:

- **Federated Averaging (FedAvg):** An algorithm to aggregate model updates from multiple clients. It averages the weights of models trained on different devices.
- **Communication Protocols:** Efficient protocols for communicating model updates, ensuring minimal bandwidth usage and secure transmission.
- **Model Aggregation:** Central server aggregates the model updates from multiple devices and sends the updated global model back to the devices.

Implementation Example:

```python
import tensorflow as tf
import tensorflow_federated as tff
```

Define a simple model

```python
def create_keras_model():
    return tf.keras.models.Sequential([
        tf.keras.layers.Dense(10, activation='relu', input_shape=(784,)),
        tf.keras.layers.Dense(10, activation='softmax')
    ])
```

Create a federated dataset

```python
federated_train_data = [tf.data.Dataset.from_tensor_slices((x, y)).batch(20) for x, y in zip(train_data, train_labels)]
```

Define a federated learning process

```python
iterative_process = tff.learning.build_federated_averaging_process(
    model_fn=create_keras_model,
    client_optimizer_fn=lambda: tf.keras.optimizers.SGD(learning_rate=0.02)
)
```

Initialize the process

```python
state = iterative_process.initialize()
```

Run the federated learning process

```python
for round in range(1, 11):
    state, metrics = iterative_process.next(state, federated_train_data)
    print('round {}, metrics={}'.format(round, metrics))
```

Privacy and Security Considerations

1. **Privacy:**

- **Differential Privacy:** Adding noise to model updates to protect individual data points.

- **Secure Aggregation:** Ensuring that the aggregation process does not expose individual model updates through techniques like secure multi-party computation.

2. **Security:**

- **Robustness Against Attacks:** Implementing measures to protect against poisoning attacks, where adversaries attempt to corrupt the model by injecting malicious data.
- **Authentication and Authorization:** Ensuring that only authorized devices can participate in the federated learning process.

Integration with Cloud Platforms

Cloud platforms provide scalable and flexible resources for deploying and managing machine learning models. Integration with cloud services allows for efficient handling of large-scale ML workloads.

Popular Cloud Services for ML

1. **AWS (Amazon Web Services):**

- **Amazon SageMaker:** A fully managed service that provides tools for building, training, and deploying machine learning models.
- **AWS Lambda:** Serverless compute service for running code in response to events, ideal for deploying lightweight ML models.
- **AWS Fargate:** A serverless compute engine for containers, suitable for deploying containerized ML applications.

2. **Google Cloud Platform (GCP):**

- **AI Platform:** Offers tools for developing, training, and deploying ML models, including AutoML and TensorFlow support.
- **BigQuery ML:** Enables the creation and execution of machine learning models directly within BigQuery using SQL.
- **Vertex AI:** A unified platform for training, deploying, and managing ML models at scale.

3. **Microsoft Azure:**

- **Azure Machine Learning:** Provides a suite of tools for building, training, and deploying ML models, with support for automated ML and MLOps.
- **Azure Cognitive Services:** Pre-built APIs for various AI capabilities like computer vision, speech recognition, and text analytics.
- **Azure Databricks:** An analytics platform optimized for Azure, ideal for big data processing and ML model training.

Implementation Example: Deploying a Model on AWS SageMaker:

```python
import sagemaker
from sagemaker import get_execution_role
from sagemaker.tensorflow import TensorFlow
role = get_execution_role()
sagemaker_session = sagemaker.Session()
```

Upload data to S3

```python
data_location = sagemaker_session.upload_data('data', key_prefix='data')
```

Define TensorFlow estimator

```python
estimator = TensorFlow(entry_point='train.py',
role=role,
instance_count=1,
instance_type='ml.m4.xlarge',
framework_version='2.3.0',
py_version='py37',
script_mode=True,
hyperparameters={'epochs': 10})
```

Train the model

```python
estimator.fit({'training': data_location})
```

Deploy the model

```python
predictor = estimator.deploy(initial_instance_count=1, instance_type='ml.m4.xlarge')
```

Make predictions

```python
predictor.predict(data)
```

Deployment Strategies and Cost Management

1. **Deployment Strategies:**

- **Blue-Green Deployment:** Deploy a new version of the model alongside the old one and gradually shift traffic from the old to the new version to ensure stability.
- **Canary Deployment:** Deploy the new model to a small subset of users to test its performance before a full rollout.
- **Shadow Deployment:** Deploy the new model in parallel with the old one, but only use the predictions for testing and not for actual decision-making.

2. **Cost Management:**

- **Spot Instances:** Use spot instances for training to reduce costs, but ensure your workload can handle interruptions.

- **Auto-scaling:** Implement auto-scaling to adjust the number of instances based on demand, ensuring cost efficiency.
- **Resource Optimization:** Regularly review and optimize resource usage, such as instance types and storage, to avoid unnecessary expenses.
- **Cost Monitoring:** Use tools like AWS Cost Explorer, Google Cloud Billing, or Azure Cost Management to monitor and control expenses.

Conclusion

This chapter has explored advanced ML systems and AI trends that are shaping the future of machine learning. Edge AI and on-device machine learning, automated machine learning, federated learning, and cloud integration are driving innovation and making ML more accessible, efficient, and secure. By understanding and leveraging these trends, you can stay ahead in the rapidly evolving field of machine learning and develop cutting-edge solutions that meet the demands of modern applications.

Chapter 6
Practical Exercises and Solutions

Designing a Social Media Monitoring System

Problem

Social media platforms generate vast amounts of data daily, including posts, comments, likes, shares, and other interactions. Monitoring this data can provide valuable insights for businesses, such as sentiment analysis, trend detection, and customer feedback analysis. The goal of this exercise is to design a social media monitoring system that can process and analyze social media data in real-time to generate actionable insights.

Step-by-Step Solution

Step 1: Define Objectives and Requirements

Objectives:

- Monitor social media platforms for specific keywords or topics.
- Perform sentiment analysis on social media posts.
- Detect trending topics and hashtags.
- Provide real-time alerts and reports.

Requirements:

- Ability to handle large volumes of data from multiple social media platforms.
- Real-time data processing and analysis.
- Scalable architecture to accommodate growing data.
- Integration with existing business intelligence tools.

Step 2: Data Collection

1. **Data Sources:**

- APIs provided by social media platforms (e.g., Twitter API, Facebook Graph API).
- Web scraping for platforms without APIs.
- Third-party data aggregators.

2. **Implementation:**

- Set up API access for social media platforms.
- Implement data collection scripts to fetch data at regular intervals.
- Store collected data in a database for further processing.

```python
import tweepy
```

Set up Twitter API access

```python
consumer_key = 'your_consumer_key'
consumer_secret = 'your_consumer_secret'
access_token = 'your_access_token'
access_token_secret = 'your_access_token_secret'
auth = tweepy.OAuthHandler(consumer_key, consumer_secret)
auth.set_access_token(access_token, access_token_secret)
api = tweepy.API(auth)
```

Fetch tweets containing a specific keyword

```python
keyword = 'your_keyword'
tweets = api.search(q=keyword, count=100)
```

Store tweets in a database

```python
import sqlite3

conn = sqlite3.connect('social_media.db')
c = conn.cursor()
c.execute('''CREATE TABLE IF NOT EXISTS tweets
(id INTEGER PRIMARY KEY, tweet TEXT, sentiment TEXT)''')
for tweet in tweets:
    c.execute("INSERT INTO tweets (tweet) VALUES (?)", (tweet.text,))
conn.commit()
conn.close()
```

Step 3: Data Preprocessing

1. **Text Cleaning:**

- Remove URLs, hashtags, mentions, and special characters.
- Convert text to lowercase.

- Remove stopwords.

2. **Sentiment Analysis:**

- Use pre-trained models or libraries like VADER, TextBlob, or transformers-based models for sentiment analysis.

```python
from textblob import TextBlob
import re
```

Function to clean tweet text

```python
def clean_tweet(tweet):
    tweet = re.sub(r'http\S+', '', tweet) # Remove URLs
    tweet = re.sub(r'@\w+', '', tweet) # Remove mentions
    tweet = re.sub(r'#\w+', '', tweet) # Remove hashtags
    tweet = re.sub(r'[^\w\s]', '', tweet) # Remove special characters
    tweet = tweet.lower() # Convert to lowercase
    return tweet
```

Function to analyze sentiment

```python
def analyze_sentiment(tweet):
    analysis = TextBlob(tweet)
    return 'positive' if analysis.sentiment.polarity > 0 else
        'negative' if analysis.sentiment.polarity < 0 else 'neutral'
```

Clean and analyze tweets

```python
conn = sqlite3.connect('social_media.db')
c = conn.cursor()
c.execute("SELECT id, tweet FROM tweets")
tweets = c.fetchall()
for tweet in tweets:
    cleaned_tweet = clean_tweet(tweet[1])
    sentiment = analyze_sentiment(cleaned_tweet)
    c.execute("UPDATE tweets SET tweet =?, sentiment =? WHERE id =?",
        (cleaned_tweet, sentiment, tweet[0]))
conn.commit()
conn.close()
```

Step 4: Trend Detection

1. **Hashtag Analysis:**

- Extract hashtags from tweets.
- Calculate the frequency of each hashtag.
- Identify trending hashtags based on frequency.

2. **Implementation:**

```python
from collections import Counter
```

Function to extract hashtags

```python
def extract_hashtags(tweet):
    return re.findall(r'#(\w+)', tweet)
```

Calculate hashtag frequencies

```python
conn = sqlite3.connect('social_media.db')
c = conn.cursor()
c.execute("SELECT tweet FROM tweets")
tweets = c.fetchall()
hashtags = []
for tweet in tweets:
hashtags.extend(extract_hashtags(tweet[0]))
hashtag_counts = Counter(hashtags)
```

Identify trending hashtags

```python
trending_hashtags = hashtag_counts.most_common(10)
print(trending_hashtags)
```

Step 5: Real-Time Alerts and Reports

1. **Real-Time Alerts:**

- Set up a system to send alerts when specific keywords or trends are detected.

2. **Reports:**

- Generate periodic reports summarizing sentiment analysis and trend detection.

Implementation:

```python
from twilio.rest import Client
Function to send SMS alerts
def send_alert(message):
client = Client('your_twilio_account_sid', 'your_twilio_auth_
    token')
client.messages.create(
to='your_phone_number',
from_='your_twilio_phone_number',
body=message
)
```

Set up a real-time monitoring system (example using a simple loop)

```python
import time
```

```python
while True:
    conn = sqlite3.connect('social_media.db')
    c = conn.cursor()
    c.execute("SELECT tweet, sentiment FROM tweets WHERE sentiment = 'negative'")
    negative_tweets = c.fetchall()
    if len(negative_tweets) > 10:  # Example threshold
    send_alert('More than 10 negative tweets detected!')
    conn.close()
    time.sleep(60)  # Check every minute
```

Building a Scalable Recommendation Engine for E-Commerce

Problem

E-commerce platforms rely on recommendation engines to suggest products to users based on their preferences and behavior. The goal of this exercise is to build a scalable recommendation engine that provides personalized product recommendations to users.

Step-by-Step Solution

Step 1: Define Objectives and Requirements

Objectives:

- Provide personalized product recommendations.
- Improve user engagement and sales.
- Scale to handle millions of users and products.

Requirements:

- Collaborative filtering and content-based filtering techniques.
- Real-time recommendations.
- Integration with the e-commerce platform.
- Scalability to handle large datasets.

Step 2: Data Collection

1. **Data Sources:**

- User interaction data (views, clicks, purchases).
- Product metadata (category, price, brand).

2. **Implementation:**

- Collect user interaction data and product metadata from the e-commerce platform's database.

```python
import pandas as pd
```

Load data

```python
user_interactions = pd.read_csv('user_interactions.csv')
product_metadata = pd.read_csv('product_metadata.csv')
```

Step 3: Data Preprocessing

1. **Data Cleaning:**

- Remove duplicate interactions.
- Handle missing values.

2. **Feature Engineering:**

- Create user and product profiles.
- Generate interaction features (e.g., purchase frequency, average rating).

Clean data

user_interactions.drop_duplicates(inplace=True)

user_interactions.fillna(0, inplace=True)

Feature engineering

user_profiles = user_interactions.groupby('user_id').agg({'product_id': 'count', 'rating': 'mean'}).reset_index()

product_profiles = product_metadata.groupby('product_id').agg({'category': 'first', 'price': 'mean', 'brand': 'first'}).reset_index()

Step 4: Model Selection and Training

1. **Collaborative Filtering:**

- Use matrix factorization techniques like Singular Value Decomposition (SVD) for user-item interaction matrix.

2. Content-Based Filtering:

- Use product metadata to recommend similar items.

Implementation:

```python
from sklearn.decomposition import TruncatedSVD
from sklearn.metrics.pairwise import cosine_similarity
```

Collaborative filtering using SVD

```python
interaction_matrix = user_interactions.pivot(index='user_id',
    columns='product_id', values='rating').fillna(0)
svd = TruncatedSVD(n_components=50)
user_factors = svd.fit_transform(interaction_matrix)
product_factors = svd.components_.T
```

Content-based filtering using cosine similarity

```python
product_similarities = cosine_similarity(product_profiles.
    drop('product_id', axis=1))
```

Combine both methods for hybrid recommendations

Step 5: Real-Time Recommendations

1. Real-Time Processing:

- Implement a recommendation engine that provides real-time product suggestions based on user interactions.

2. API Development:

- Develop an API to serve recommendations to the e-commerce platform.

Implementation:

```python
from flask import Flask, request, jsonify
app = Flask(__name__)
@app.route('/recommend', methods=['POST'])
def recommend():
user_id = request.json['user_id']
```

Generate recommendations using collaborative and content-based filtering

```python
recommendations = generate_recommendations(user_id)
return jsonify(recommendations)
def generate_recommendations(user_id):
```

Implement recommendation logic here

```python
pass
```

```
if __name__ == '__main__':
    app.run(debug=True)
```

Develop a Real-Time Anomaly Detection System

Problem Description

Anomaly detection systems identify unusual patterns in data that do not conform to expected behavior. This exercise focuses on developing a real-time anomaly detection system for a financial institution to detect fraudulent transactions.

Step-by-Step Solution

Step 1: Define Objectives and Requirements

Objectives:

- Detect fraudulent transactions in real-time.
- Minimize false positives and false negatives.
- Provide actionable alerts for detected anomalies.

Requirements:

- Ability to process transactions in real-time.
- Scalable architecture to handle large volumes of transactions.
- Integration with existing financial systems.
- Robust model to handle evolving fraud patterns.

Step 2: Data Collection

1. **Data Sources:**

- Transaction data (amount, location, time, merchant).
- User data (account details, transaction history).

2. **Implementation:**

- Collect transaction and user data from the financial institution's database.

```python
import pandas as pd
```

Load data

```python
transactions = pd.read_csv('transactions.csv')
user_data = pd.read_csv('user_data.csv')
```

Step 3: Data Preprocessing

1. **Data Cleaning:**

- Handle missing values.
- Remove duplicate transactions.

2. **Feature Engineering:**

- Create features that capture patterns indicative of fraud (e.g., transaction frequency, amount deviations).

Clean data

```python
transactions.fillna(0, inplace=True)
transactions.drop_duplicates(inplace=True)
```

Feature engineering

```python
transactions['transaction_hour'] = pd.to_datetime(transactions['transaction_time']).dt.hour
user_profiles = user_data.groupby('user_id').agg({'transaction_id': 'count', 'amount': 'mean'}).reset_index()
```

Step 4: Model Selection and Training

1. **Anomaly Detection Models:**

- Use models like Isolation Forest, One-Class SVM, or LSTM for sequence data.

2. **Training the Model:**

- Train the model on historical transaction data.

Implementation:

```python
from sklearn.ensemble import IsolationForest
from sklearn.preprocessing import StandardScaler
```

Normalize data

```python
scaler = StandardScaler()
scaled_transactions = scaler.fit_transform(transactions[['amount', 'transaction_hour']])
```

Train Isolation Forest model
```
model = IsolationForest(contamination=0.01)
model.fit(scaled_transactions)
```
Predict anomalies
```
transactions['anomaly'] = model.predict(scaled_transactions)
```

Step 5: Real-Time Processing and Alerts

1. **Real-Time Processing:**

- Implement a real-time anomaly detection system that processes transactions as they occur.

2. **Alerts:**

- Set up a system to send alerts when anomalies are detected.

Implementation:
```
from flask import Flask, request, jsonify
app = Flask(__name__)
model = IsolationForest(contamination=0.01)
model.fit(scaled_transactions) Pre-trained model
@app.route('/detect_anomaly', methods=['POST'])
def detect_anomaly():
transaction = request.json['transaction']
scaled_transaction = scaler.transform([transaction['amount'],
   transaction['transaction_hour']])
anomaly = model.predict(scaled_transaction)
return jsonify({'anomaly': bool(anomaly)})
if __name__ == '__main__':
app.run(debug=True)
```

Create a Predictive Maintenance System

Problem Description

Predictive maintenance systems use data to predict equipment failures before they occur, allowing for timely maintenance and reducing downtime. This exercise focuses on developing a predictive maintenance system for a manufacturing plant.

Step-by-Step Solution

Step 1: Define Objectives and Requirements

Objectives:

- Predict equipment failures before they occur.
- Reduce downtime and maintenance costs.
- Improve overall equipment efficiency.

Requirements:

- Ability to process sensor data in real-time.
- Scalable architecture to handle large volumes of data from multiple machines.
- Integration with existing maintenance systems.
- Accurate and robust predictive models.

Step 2: Data Collection

1. **Data Sources:**

- Sensor data from machines (temperature, vibration, pressure).
- Maintenance logs.

2. **Implementation:**

- Collect sensor data and maintenance logs from the manufacturing plant's database.

    ```
    import pandas as pd
    ```

Load data

```python
sensor_data = pd.read_csv('sensor_data.csv')
maintenance_logs = pd.read_csv('maintenance_logs.csv')
```

Step 3: Data Preprocessing

1. **Data Cleaning:**

- Handle missing values.
- Remove duplicate records.

2. **Feature Engineering:**

- Create features that capture patterns indicative of equipment failure (e.g., average temperature, vibration peaks).

Clean data

```python
sensor_data.fillna(0, inplace=True)
sensor_data.drop_duplicates(inplace=True)
```

Feature engineering

```python
sensor_data['temperature_avg'] = sensor_data.groupby('machine_id')
    ['temperature'].transform('mean')
sensor_data['vibration_peaks'] = sensor_data['vibration'].apply(lambda
    x: len([i for i in x if i > threshold]))
```

Step 4: Model Selection and Training

1. **Predictive Models:**

- Use models like Random Forest, Gradient Boosting, or LSTM for time series data.

2. **Training the Model:**

- Train the model on historical sensor data and maintenance logs.

Implementation:

```python
from sklearn.ensemble import RandomForestClassifier
from sklearn.model_selection import train_test_split
```

Prepare data

```python
X = sensor_data.drop(['failure'], axis=1)
y = sensor_data['failure']
```

Train-test split

```python
X_train, X_test, y_train, y_test = train_test_split(X, y, test_
    size=0.2, random_state=42)
```

Train Random Forest model

```
model = RandomForestClassifier()
model.fit(X_train, y_train)
```

Evaluate the model

```
y_pred = model.predict(X_test)
accuracy = accuracy_score(y_test, y_pred)
print(f"Accuracy: {accuracy}")
```

Step 5: Real-Time Processing and Alerts

1. **Real-Time Processing:**

- Implement a predictive maintenance system that processes sensor data in real-time to predict equipment failures.

2. **Alerts:**

- Set up a system to send alerts when potential failures are detected.

Implementation:

```
from flask import Flask, request, jsonify
app = Flask(__name__)
model = RandomForestClassifier()
model.fit(X_train, y_train) Pre-trained model
@app.route('/predict_failure', methods=['POST'])
def predict_failure():
sensor_data = request.json['sensor_data']
prediction = model.predict([sensor_data])
return jsonify({'failure': bool(prediction)})
if __name__ == '__main__':
app.run(debug=True)
```

Conclusion

This chapter provides practical exercises and solutions for designing and implementing various machine learning systems. By working through these examples, you will gain hands-on experience in building social media monitoring systems, recommendation engines, anomaly detection systems, and predictive maintenance systems. Each exercise includes problem statements, step-by-step solutions, and practical implementation examples to guide you through the process.

Chapter 7
Industry Insights and Expert Interviews

Insights from Top ML Engineers

Interviews with Industry Leaders

1. **Introduction to Interviews:**

- The field of machine learning (ML) is rapidly evolving, and staying ahead requires insights from those at the forefront. In this section, we present interviews with leading ML engineers and researchers who share their experiences, challenges, and predictions for the future of ML.

Interview 1: Dr. Jane Doe, Chief Data Scientist at AI Innovators Inc.

Q1: Can you tell us about your journey into machine learning and your current role?
Dr. Jane Doe: My journey into ML began during my undergraduate studies in computer science. I was fascinated by the potential of algorithms to learn from data and make predictions. After completing my Ph.D. in machine learning, I joined AI Innovators Inc. as a data scientist. Today, as the Chief Data Scientist, I lead a team of researchers and engineers working on cutting-edge ML projects, including autonomous systems and healthcare applications.

Q2: What are some of the biggest challenges you face in your work? Dr. Jane Doe: One of the biggest challenges is ensuring the ethical use of AI. This includes addressing biases in data, ensuring transparency in models, and making sure our AI systems are fair and unbiased. Another challenge is scalability—building models that can handle massive datasets and provide real-time predictions is no small feat.

Q3: What trends do you see shaping the future of ML? Dr. Jane Doe: I see a few key trends emerging. First, there's a growing emphasis on explainable AI, where models are designed to be interpretable. Second, edge computing is becoming more prevalent, allowing ML models to run on devices with limited resources. Finally, federated learning is gaining traction, enabling decentralized model training while preserving data privacy.

Interview 2: John Smith, Senior ML Engineer at TechCorp

Q1: How did you get started in machine learning? John Smith: My interest in ML started during my master's program in data science. I worked on a project involving natural language processing (NLP) and was hooked. After graduation, I joined TechCorp as an ML engineer, where I've been working on various projects, from recommendation systems to fraud detection.

Q2: What are the most exciting projects you've worked on? John Smith: One of the most exciting projects was developing a real-time fraud detection system for our payment platform. It involved working with massive datasets and designing models that could detect fraudulent transactions with high accuracy. Another project was an NLP-based chatbot that improved customer service by providing instant responses to common queries.

Q3: What advice would you give to aspiring ML engineers? John Smith: Stay curious and keep learning. ML is a rapidly evolving field, and new techniques and tools are constantly emerging. Participate in online courses, attend conferences, and contribute to open-source projects. Also, focus on building a strong foundation in mathematics and programming, as these skills are essential for success in ML.

Key Trends and Future Directions

1. **Explainable AI:**
   - Explainable AI (XAI) focuses on making ML models interpretable and transparent. This trend is crucial for gaining trust from stakeholders and ensuring ethical AI use. Techniques like SHAP (SHapley Additive exPlanations) and LIME (Local Interpretable Model-agnostic Explanations) are becoming standard tools for interpreting complex models.

2. **Edge Computing:**
   - Edge computing enables ML models to run on devices with limited resources, such as smartphones and IoT devices. This trend reduces latency and enhances privacy by processing data locally. Innovations in hardware, like NVIDIA's Jetson and Google's Coral, are driving this shift towards edge AI.

3. **Federated Learning:**
   - Federated learning allows models to be trained across decentralized devices without sharing raw data. This approach enhances privacy and security, making it ideal for applications in healthcare and finance. Companies like Google and Apple are already implementing federated learning in their products.

4. **AutoML:**
   - Automated machine learning (AutoML) simplifies the ML workflow by automating

tasks like feature selection, model selection, and hyperparameter tuning. This trend democratizes ML by making it accessible to non-experts. Tools like Google's AutoML and H2O.ai's Driverless AI are leading the way.

5. **AI Ethics and Fairness:**

- As AI becomes more integrated into society, ensuring ethical use and fairness is paramount. Researchers are developing frameworks to identify and mitigate biases in data and models. Regulatory bodies are also creating guidelines to ensure that AI systems are fair and transparent.

Preparing for a Career in ML

Career Pathways and Opportunities

1. **Overview of Career Pathways:**

- Machine learning offers diverse career opportunities across various industries, including technology, healthcare, finance, and retail. Career pathways include roles such as data scientist, ML engineer, research scientist, and AI specialist.

2. **Data Scientist:**

- Data scientists analyze and interpret complex data to provide insights and support decision-making. They use statistical techniques and machine learning algorithms to identify patterns and build predictive models. Key skills include programming (Python, R), data wrangling, and visualization.

3. **ML Engineer:**

- ML engineers design and deploy machine learning models in production environments. They work on model training, optimization, and integration with other systems. Essential skills include software engineering, deep learning frameworks (TensorFlow, PyTorch), and MLOps practices.

4. **Research Scientist:**

- Research scientists focus on advancing the state of the art in machine learning through theoretical and applied research. They publish papers, develop new algorithms, and collaborate with academic institutions. A strong academic background and expertise in a specific ML domain are crucial.

5. **AI Specialist:**

- AI specialists work on developing and implementing AI solutions for specific applications, such as computer vision, NLP, or robotics. They combine domain knowledge with technical expertise to solve complex problems. Key skills include specialized ML techniques, domain knowledge, and problem-solving abilities.

Continuous Learning and Skills Development

1. **Importance of Lifelong Learning:**
- The field of ML is dynamic and continuously evolving. Lifelong learning is essential to stay updated with the latest advancements, tools, and techniques. Engaging in continuous learning helps professionals maintain their competitive edge and adapt to new challenges.

2. **Online Courses and Certifications:**
- Numerous online platforms offer courses and certifications in machine learning, data science, and AI. Popular platforms include Coursera, edX, Udacity, and Khan Academy. Certifications from reputable institutions and companies (e.g., Google's TensorFlow Developer Certificate) can enhance your resume.

3. **Reading Research Papers:**
- Reading research papers from conferences like NeurIPS, ICML, and CVPR helps you stay informed about cutting-edge developments. Platforms like arXiv and Google Scholar are excellent resources for accessing the latest research.

4. **Participating in ML Competitions:**
- Competitions on platforms like Kaggle and DrivenData provide hands-on experience with real-world datasets and problems. They also offer opportunities to collaborate with other ML practitioners and gain recognition in the community.

5. **Attending Conferences and Workshops:**
- Attending industry conferences, workshops, and meetups allows you to network with experts, learn about new trends, and gain insights from presentations and discussions. Notable conferences include NeurIPS, ICML, and Strata Data Conference.

Navigating the Job Market

Effective Job Search Strategies

1. **Identifying Job Opportunities:**
- Leverage job boards, company websites, and professional networks to find job open-

ings in machine learning. Popular job boards include LinkedIn, Indeed, and Glassdoor. Companies like Google, Facebook, Amazon, and Microsoft frequently post ML-related positions.

2. **Tailoring Your Resume and Cover Letter:**

- Customize your resume and cover letter for each application. Highlight relevant skills, projects, and experiences that align with the job requirements. Use specific keywords and phrases from the job description to pass through applicant tracking systems (ATS).

3. **Building a Strong Online Presence:**

- Maintain a professional online presence on platforms like LinkedIn and GitHub. Share your projects, publications, and achievements. Write articles or blog posts about your work and participate in discussions related to ML and AI.

4. **Preparing for Technical Interviews:**

- Technical interviews for ML positions often include coding challenges, algorithm design, and ML-specific questions. Practice coding on platforms like LeetCode and HackerRank. Review key ML concepts and algorithms, and be prepared to discuss your projects and experiences in detail.

Networking and Building One's Professional Brand

1. **Importance of Networking:**

- Networking is crucial for career growth in machine learning. Building connections with professionals in the field can lead to job opportunities, collaborations, and mentorship. Attend industry events, join online communities, and engage with peers on social media.

2. **Joining Professional Organizations:**

- Professional organizations like IEEE, ACM, and Data Science Society offer networking opportunities, resources, and events for ML practitioners. Membership in these organizations can enhance your professional brand and provide access to valuable resources.

3. **Participating in Open Source Projects:**

- Contributing to open-source projects on platforms like GitHub can showcase your skills and expertise to potential employers. It also allows you to collaborate with other developers and learn from their experiences.

4. **Building a Personal Brand:**

- Establish yourself as an expert in machine learning by sharing your knowledge and insights. Write blog posts, give talks at conferences, and create video tutorials. Consistently sharing high-quality content can help you build a strong professional brand.

5. **Seeking Mentorship:**

- Finding a mentor in the ML field can provide guidance, support, and valuable insights. Reach out to experienced professionals, join mentorship programs, and participate in networking events to connect with potential mentors.

Conclusion

This chapter provides industry insights and expert interviews, highlighting key trends and future directions in machine learning. It also offers practical advice on preparing for a career in ML, including career pathways, continuous learning, and navigating the job market. By following these strategies and building a strong professional brand, you can enhance your career prospects and succeed in the dynamic field of machine learning.

Chapter 8
Comprehensive Preparation Tools

Quick Reference Sheets

Quick reference sheets are essential tools that help you recall important information quickly. They condense key concepts, algorithms, and techniques into an easily digestible format. Here, we provide reference sheets for various aspects of machine learning and system design.

Key ML Algorithms

1. **Supervised Learning:**

- **Linear Regression:**
- **Equation:** $y = \beta_0 + \beta_1 x + \epsilon$
- **Use Case:** Predicting continuous outcomes (e.g., house prices).
- **Key Points:** Assumes a linear relationship, sensitive to outliers.
- **Logistic Regression:**
- **Equation:** $\text{logit}(p) = \ln\left(\frac{p}{1-p}\right) = \beta_0 + \beta_1 x$
- **Use Case:** Binary classification (e.g., spam detection).
- **Key Points:** Outputs probabilities, uses sigmoid function.
- **Decision Trees:**
- **Structure:** Tree-like model of decisions.
- **Use Case:** Both classification and regression.
- **Key Points:** Easy to interpret, prone to overfitting.
- **Random Forest:**
- **Concept:** Ensemble of decision trees.
- **Use Case:** Classification and regression.
- **Key Points:** Reduces overfitting, handles missing values well.
- **Support Vector Machines (SVM):**
- **Equation:** $f(x) = \text{sign}(w \cdot x + b)$
- **Use Case:** Classification, especially for high-dimensional data.
- **Key Points:** Effective in high-dimensional spaces, can use different kernel functions.

2. **Unsupervised Learning:**

- **K-Means Clustering:**
- **Objective:** Partition data into K clusters.
- **Use Case:** Market segmentation, image compression.
- **Key Points:** Sensitive to initial cluster centers, requires specifying K.
- **Principal Component Analysis (PCA):**
- **Objective:** Reduce dimensionality by transforming data to principal components.
- **Use Case:** Data visualization, noise reduction.
- **Key Points:** Maximizes variance, linear transformation.
- **Autoencoders:**
- **Structure:** Neural network used for unsupervised learning of efficient codings.
- **Use Case:** Anomaly detection, data denoising.
- **Key Points:** Consists of encoder and decoder parts, can handle nonlinear transformations.

3. **Deep Learning:**

- **Convolutional Neural Networks (CNNs):**
- **Structure:** Multiple layers of convolutions and pooling.
- **Use Case:** Image recognition, object detection.
- **Key Points:** Captures spatial hierarchies, effective for grid-like data.
- **Recurrent Neural Networks (RNNs):**
- **Structure:** Recurrent connections in the network.
- **Use Case:** Sequence prediction, language modeling.
- **Key Points:** Handles sequential data, suffers from vanishing gradient problem (mitigated by LSTM/GRU).

Evaluation Metrics

1. **Classification Metrics:**

- **Accuracy:** $\frac{\text{TP} + \text{TN}}{\text{TP} + \text{TN} + \text{FP} + \text{FN}}$
- **Use Case:** Balanced classes.
- **Precision:** $\frac{\text{TP}}{\text{TP} + \text{FP}}$
- **Use Case:** Focus on minimizing false positives.
- **Recall (Sensitivity):** $\frac{\text{TP}}{\text{TP} + \text{FN}}$
- **Use Case:** Focus on minimizing false negatives.
- **F1 Score:** $2 \times \frac{\text{Precision} \times \text{Recall}}{\text{Precision} + \text{Recall}}$
- **Use Case:** Balance between precision and recall.
- **ROC-AUC:** Area under the Receiver Operating Characteristic curve.
- **Use Case:** Evaluate binary classifiers.

2. **Regression Metrics:**

- **Mean Squared Error (MSE):** $\frac{1}{n} \sum_{i=1}^{n} (y_i - \hat{y}_i)^2$
- **Use Case:** Penalizes large errors.
- **Mean Absolute Error (MAE):** $\frac{1}{n} \sum_{i=1}^{n} |y_i - \hat{y}_i|$
- **Use Case:** More robust to outliers.
- **R-squared:** $1 - \frac{\sum_{i=1}^{n} (y_i - \hat{y}_i)^2}{\sum_{i=1}^{n} (y_i - \bar{y})^2}$
- **Use Case:** Proportion of variance explained by the model.

3. **Clustering Metrics:**

- **Silhouette Score:** Measures how similar an object is to its own cluster compared to other clusters.
- **Use Case:** Evaluate cluster cohesion and separation.
- **Davies-Bouldin Index:** Measures the average similarity ratio of each cluster with the cluster most similar to it.
- **Use Case:** Lower values indicate better clustering.

Common Interview Questions and How to Address Them

Technical Questions

1. **Explain the bias-variance tradeoff.**

- **Response:** The bias-variance tradeoff is a fundamental concept in ML that describes the tradeoff between the error introduced by the bias and the variance of the model. High bias can cause underfitting, where the model is too simple to capture the underlying pattern. High variance can cause overfitting, where the model captures noise along with the pattern.

2. **What is cross-validation, and why is it important?**

- **Response:** Cross-validation is a technique for assessing the performance of a model by training and testing it on different subsets of the data. It helps ensure that the model generalizes well to unseen data and is not overfitting. Common methods include k-fold cross-validation and leave-one-out cross-validation.

3. **How does a decision tree algorithm work?**

- **Response:** A decision tree algorithm splits the data into subsets based on the feature that results in the highest information gain or the lowest Gini impurity. Each node represents a feature, each branch represents a decision rule, and each leaf represents an outcome. The process continues recursively until the stopping criteria are met.

4. **What are the differences between L1 and L2 regularization?**

- **Response:** L1 regularization adds the absolute value of the coefficients to the loss function, promoting sparsity (many coefficients become zero). L2 regularization adds the squared value of the coefficients to the loss function, promoting smaller but non-zero coefficients. L1 is useful for feature selection, while L2 is useful for preventing overfitting.

5. **How would you handle imbalanced datasets?**

- **Response:** Handling imbalanced datasets can involve techniques like:
- **Resampling:** Oversampling the minority class or undersampling the majority class.
- **Synthetic Data Generation:** Using methods like SMOTE to create synthetic examples.
- **Adjusting Class Weights:** Modifying the loss function to penalize misclassifications of the minority class more heavily.
- **Ensemble Methods:** Combining multiple models to improve performance on the minority class.

Behavioral Questions

1. **Describe a challenging project you worked on and how you managed it.**

- **Response:** Use the STAR method (Situation, Task, Action, Result) to structure your answer. Describe the project's context, your specific role, the steps you took to address the challenges, and the outcome of your efforts.

2. **How do you stay updated with the latest developments in ML?**

- **Response:** Mention specific resources you use, such as academic journals, conferences, online courses, and industry blogs. Highlight any active participation in the ML community, such as contributing to open-source projects or attending meetups.

3. **How do you approach problem-solving in your projects?**

- **Response:** Describe your problem-solving process, including understanding the problem, breaking it down into manageable parts, researching potential solutions, experimenting with different approaches, and iterating based on feedback.

4. **Can you describe a time when you had to work with a difficult team member?**

- **Response:** Use the STAR method to describe the situation, your role, the specific actions you took to address the issue, and the positive outcome. Emphasize your communication and conflict-resolution skills.

5. **How do you handle tight deadlines and pressure?**

- **Response:** Explain your time-management strategies, such as prioritizing tasks, setting realistic goals, and maintaining clear communication with stakeholders. Provide an example of a past experience where you successfully managed a high-pressure situation.

Checklists for the Day of the Interview

Pre-Interview Preparation

1. **Review Key Concepts:**

- Refresh your knowledge of key ML concepts, algorithms, and techniques.
- Practice coding problems and system design scenarios.

2. **Research the Company:**

- Understand the company's products, services, and recent news.
- Identify how your skills and experiences align with the company's needs.

3. **Prepare Your Questions:**

- Have thoughtful questions ready to ask the interviewer about the role, team, and company culture.

4. **Plan Your Route:**

- Ensure you know the exact location of the interview and plan your route.
- Allow extra time for potential delays.

5. **Gather Necessary Materials:**

- Bring multiple copies of your resume.
- Have a notebook and pen for taking notes.
- Ensure any required identification or documents are prepared.

During the Interview

1. **Dress Appropriately:**

- Wear professional attire that is appropriate for the company's culture.

2. **Arrive Early:**

- Aim to arrive at least 10-15 minutes early.

3. **Be Confident and Courteous:**

- Greet everyone you meet with a smile and a firm handshake.
- Maintain eye contact and positive body language.

4. **Listen Carefully:**

- Listen to the interviewer's questions attentively.
- Take a moment to think before responding if needed.

5. **Provide Clear and Concise Answers:**

- Use the STAR method for behavioral questions.
- Be specific about your technical knowledge and experiences.

6. **Ask Insightful Questions:**

- Show your interest in the role and the company by asking relevant questions.

Follow-Up After the Interview

1. **Send a Thank-You Email:**

- Send a personalized thank-you email to each interviewer within 24 hours.
- Express your appreciation for the opportunity and reiterate your interest in the position.

2. **Reflect on the Interview:**

- Assess your performance and identify areas for improvement.
- Note any questions you found challenging and review the answers.

3. **Follow Up:**

- If you haven't heard back within the expected timeframe, send a polite follow-up email to inquire about the status of your application.

Conclusion

Summary of key concepts

In this book we have explored the intricate world of machine learning (ML) and system design, providing a comprehensive guide to mastering the concepts and skills needed to succeed in this field. We summarize the key concepts covered in each chapter:

1. **Introduction to ML systems design interviews:**

- Importance of ML systems design interviews.
- Structured approach to preparing for these interviews.
- Latest trends and advances in the ML field.

2. **The 6-step approach to ML system design:**

- **Problem understanding:** clear definition of the problem and its scope, understanding of business objectives, and requirements gathering.
- **Data collection and pre-processing:** Identification of data sources, data collection and pre-processing to ensure data quality and consistency.
- **Model selection and training:** Choosing the right model based on the type of problem, data characteristics and project requirements; training the model according to best practices.
- **Model evaluation and validation:** Evaluation of model performance using appropriate metrics and cross-validation techniques.
- **Deployment and monitoring:** Implementing the model in a production environment; setting up monitoring to ensure consistent performance.
- **Iteration and improvement:** Continuously improve the model based on feedback and new data, implementing experimentation and innovation.

3. **Fundamental concepts and best practices:**

- **Data preprocessing and feature engineering:** Handling missing data, scaling and normalization of features, coding of categorical variables.
- **Model selection and hyperparameter adjustment:** Appropriate model selection, hyperparameter optimization using techniques such as grid search and random search.
- **Model evaluation and validation metrics:** Understanding and applying metrics such as accuracy, precision, recall, F1 score, ROC-AUC, confusion matrix and regression metrics.
- **Scalability and performance optimization:** Implementation of distributed and parallel processing, data pipeline optimization.

- **Ethics and fairness in ML:** Identifying and mitigating bias, ensuring transparency and explainability.

4. **Real-world case studies:**

- Detailed case studies on the design of a visual search system, real-time content recommendation engine, advanced fraud detection system, and personalized health predictions.
- Problem solving, data collection and pre-processing, model selection and training, implementation and monitoring, key lessons and insights.

5. **Advanced ML systems and AI trends.**

- **Edge AI and On-Device Machine Learning:** Architectures, Use Cases, Benefits and Challenges.
- **Machine Learning (AutoML):** Tools, techniques, applications and best practices.
- **Federated Learning Systems:** Principles, implementation, privacy and security considerations.
- **Integration with cloud platforms:** Popular cloud services, implementation strategies, cost management.

6. **Hands-on exercises and solutions:**

- Step-by-step solutions for designing a social media monitoring system, building a scalable recommendation engine, developing a real-time anomaly detection system, and creating a predictive maintenance system.
- Problem description, data collection and pre-processing, model selection and training, real-time processing and alerts.

7. **Industry insights and expert interviews:**

- Insights from top ML engineers and industry leaders.
- Key trends and future directions of ML.
- Preparation for a ML career: career paths, continuous learning, navigating the job market, networking, and building a professional brand.

8. **Comprehensive preparation tools:**

- Quick reference sheets, common interview questions and how to address them.
- Checklists for the day of the interview: preparation before the interview, during the interview, follow-up after the interview.
- Online resources and additional reading materials.

Encouragement for continuous learning and development

The field of machine learning is dynamic and constantly evolving. To stay relevant and successful, you need to engage in continuous learning and development. Here are some key strategies to help you on this journey:

1. **Embrace continuous learning:**

- Stay curious: Always be curious and open to learning new things. The more you learn, the more competent and adaptable you will become.
- **Online courses and certifications:** Take advantage of online courses and certifications to improve your knowledge and skills. Platforms such as Coursera, edX, Udacity and Khan Academy offer valuable resources.

2. **Keep abreast of industry trends:**

- Read **research papers:** Stay up-to-date on the latest research by reading papers from conferences such as NeurIPS, ICML and CVPR. Platforms such as arXiv and Google Scholar are excellent resources.
- **Follow blogs and industry news:** Subscribe to blogs and industry news sources such as Towards Data Science, KDnuggets, Distill and Analytics Vidhya.

3. **Gain hands-on experience:**

- **Participate in competitions:** Participate in ML competitions on platforms such as Kaggle and DrivenData to gain hands-on experience and solve real problems.
- **Work on projects:** Build your own projects to apply your knowledge and showcase your skills. Document your work and share it on platforms such as GitHub.

4. **Network and collaborate:**

- Attend **conferences and meetings:** Attend industry conferences, workshops and meetings to network with experts and colleagues.
- **Participate** in online communities: Participate in online communities and forums such as Reddit, Stack Overflow, and Data Science Stack Exchange.

5. **Seek mentors:**

- **Find a mentor:** Connect with experienced professionals who can provide guidance, support, and insights.
- **Mentor others:** Share your knowledge and experience by mentoring others. Teaching is a great way to reinforce your own learning.

Final tips for success

Success in machine learning requires a combination of technical skills, practical experience, and personal qualities. Here are some final tips to help you succeed:

1. **Build a solid foundation:**
   - **Master the basics:** Make sure you have a solid grasp of the fundamental concepts of mathematics, statistics and computer science. These are the building blocks of machine learning.
   - **Develop programming skills:** Knowledge of programming languages such as Python and R and tools such as TensorFlow and PyTorch is essential.

2. **Focus on problem solving:**
   - **Understand the problem:** Take the time to understand the problem you are trying to solve. Clear problem definition and requirements gathering are crucial steps.
   - **Think critically:** Apply critical thinking and analytical skills to break down complex problems and develop effective solutions.

3. **Communicate effectively:**
   - **Technical communication:** Be able to explain complex technical concepts clearly and concisely to technical and non-technical audiences.
   - **Collaboration:** Work effectively with cross-functional teams, sharing ideas and feedback constructively.

4. **Resilience and adaptation:**
   - **Embrace failure:** Learn from failures and setbacks. Every mistake is an opportunity to grow and improve.
   - **Adapt to change:** The ML field is constantly evolving. Stay flexible and be willing to adapt to new tools, techniques, and methodologies.

5. **Maintain ethical standards:**
   - **Ethical considerations:** Ensure that your work in machine learning is ethical and responsible. Address bias, ensure fairness and maintain transparency in your models.
   - **Social impact:** Consider the broader impact of your work on society. Try to develop solutions that benefit everyone.

6. **Plan long-term goals:**
   - **Set clear goals:** Define your long-term career goals and create a roadmap to achieve them. Set milestones and evaluate your progress regularly.
   - **Seek continuous improvement:** Always seek to improve your skills, knowledge and performance.

In conclusion, mastering machine learning and systems design is a challenging but rewarding journey. This book has provided you with the tools, knowledge, and strategies you need to successfully navigate this journey. Keep learning, keep being curious, and keep pushing the boundaries of what is possible with machine learning. Your dedication and passion will lead you to achieve great things in this exciting field.

Appendix

Glossary of Terms

Accuracy: A metric for evaluating classification models, calculated as the ratio of correctly predicted instances to the total instances. It is useful for balanced datasets but can be misleading with imbalanced classes.

Algorithm: A step-by-step procedure or formula for solving a problem. In machine learning, algorithms are used to learn patterns from data and make predictions.

Anomaly Detection: The process of identifying rare or unusual patterns that do not conform to expected behavior. It is commonly used for fraud detection, network security, and fault detection.

AutoML (Automated Machine Learning): A set of tools and techniques that automate the end-to-end process of applying machine learning to real-world problems. AutoML includes tasks like data preprocessing, model selection, hyperparameter tuning, and model evaluation.

Bias: In machine learning, bias refers to the error introduced by approximating a real-world problem, which may be complex, by a simplified model. High bias can cause underfitting, where the model is too simple to capture the underlying pattern in the data.

Cross-Validation: A technique for assessing the performance of a model by training and testing it on different subsets of the data. It helps ensure that the model generalizes well to unseen data. Common methods include k-fold cross-validation and leave-one-out cross-validation.

Data Preprocessing: The process of preparing raw data for analysis by cleaning, transforming, and organizing it. This step is crucial for ensuring data quality and improving the performance of machine learning models.

Deep Learning: A subset of machine learning that involves neural networks with many layers. Deep learning models are capable of learning complex patterns in large datasets and are commonly used in image and speech recognition, natural language processing, and autonomous systems.

Dimensionality Reduction: Techniques used to reduce the number of features in a dataset while retaining as much information as possible. Common methods include Principal Component Analysis (PCA) and t-Distributed Stochastic Neighbor Embedding (t-SNE).

Evaluation Metrics: Measures used to assess the performance of a machine learning model. Common metrics include accuracy, precision, recall, F1 score, mean squared error, and ROC-AUC.

Feature Engineering: The process of creating new features or modifying existing ones to improve the performance of machine learning models. This step often requires domain knowledge and creativity.

Federated Learning: A decentralized approach to training machine learning models where data remains on the local devices, and only model updates are shared. This approach enhances privacy and allows for the utilization of data from various sources without centralizing it.

Hyperparameter Tuning: The process of optimizing the hyperparameters of a machine learning model to improve its performance. Common techniques include grid search, random search, and Bayesian optimization.

K-Means Clustering: An unsupervised learning algorithm that partitions data into KKK clusters by minimizing the distance between data points and the centroid of the clusters.

L1 Regularization (Lasso): A regularization technique that adds the absolute value of the coefficients to the loss function. It promotes sparsity, meaning many coefficients become zero, which can be useful for feature selection.

L2 Regularization (Ridge): A regularization technique that adds the squared value of the coefficients to the loss function. It promotes smaller but non-zero coefficients, which helps prevent overfitting.

Logistic Regression: A statistical model used for binary classification problems. It uses the logistic function to model the probability of a binary outcome based on one or more predictor variables.

Machine Learning (ML): A subset of artificial intelligence that involves training algorithms to learn patterns from data and make predictions or decisions without being explicitly programmed.

Model Deployment: The process of integrating a trained machine learning model into a production environment where it can make predictions on new data.

Model Evaluation: The process of assessing the performance of a machine learning model using metrics and validation techniques to ensure it generalizes well to unseen data.

Model Overfitting: A scenario where a machine learning model learns the training data too well, including noise and outliers, resulting in poor generalization to new data.

Model Underfitting: A scenario where a machine learning model is too simple to capture the underlying pattern in the data, resulting in poor performance on both the training and new data.

Neural Network: A computational model inspired by the human brain, consisting of interconnected nodes (neurons) organized in layers. Neural networks are used in deep learning to learn complex patterns from data.

Overfitting: When a model learns the training data too well, including noise and outliers, resulting in poor performance on new, unseen data. Techniques like regularization, cross-validation, and pruning can help mitigate overfitting.

Precision: A metric for evaluating classification models, calculated as the ratio of true positive predictions to the total positive predictions. Precision measures the model's ability to correctly identify positive instances.

Recall: A metric for evaluating classification models, calculated as the ratio of true positive predictions to the total actual positives. Recall measures the model's ability to capture all relevant positive instances.

Regression: A type of supervised learning used to predict continuous outcomes based on one or more predictor variables. Common algorithms include linear regression, ridge regression, and Lasso regression.

ROC-AUC (Receiver Operating Characteristic - Area Under the Curve): A performance metric for binary classification models, plotting the true positive rate against the false positive rate at various threshold settings. The area under the ROC curve (AUC) provides a measure of the model's ability to distinguish between classes.

Scalability: The ability of a machine learning system to handle increasing amounts of data and computational workload efficiently.

Supervised Learning: A type of machine learning where the algorithm is trained on labeled data, meaning the input data is paired with the correct output. Common tasks include classification and regression.

Support Vector Machine (SVM): A supervised learning algorithm used for classification and regression tasks. It finds the optimal hyperplane that separates data points of different classes with the maximum margin.

Unsupervised Learning: A type of machine learning where the algorithm is trained on unlabeled data, meaning the input data has no corresponding output. Common tasks include clustering and dimensionality reduction.

Validation Set: A subset of the dataset used to tune hyperparameters and select the best model during the training process. It helps prevent overfitting by providing an unbiased evaluation of the model's performance.

Variance: In machine learning, variance refers to the error introduced by the model's sensitivity to small fluctuations in the training data. High variance can cause overfitting, where the model learns the noise along with the underlying pattern.

XGBoost: An optimized gradient boosting framework that uses decision trees for classification and regression tasks. It is known for its speed and performance, often used in ML competitions.

Additional Resources and Recommended Readings

Books:

1. **"Hands-On Machine Learning with Scikit-Learn, Keras, and TensorFlow" by Aurélien Géron:**

- This practical guide covers machine learning using Python libraries. It is ideal for beginners and intermediate practitioners, providing hands-on examples and clear explanations.

2. **"Deep Learning" by Ian Goodfellow, Yoshua Bengio, and Aaron Courville:**

- A comprehensive textbook on deep learning, covering theory and practice. It is suitable for advanced practitioners and researchers looking to deepen their understanding of deep learning techniques.

3. **"Pattern Recognition and Machine Learning" by Christopher Bishop:**

- An in-depth introduction to pattern recognition and machine learning algorithms. This book is recommended for those with a strong mathematical background.

4. **"The Hundred-Page Machine Learning Book" by Andriy Burkov:**

- A concise overview of essential machine learning concepts and techniques. It is a great resource for quick reference and review.

5. **"Machine Learning Yearning" by Andrew Ng:**

- This book provides practical advice on how to structure machine learning projects and tackle common challenges. It is particularly useful for those managing ML teams and projects.

Online Courses and Platforms:

1. **Coursera:**

- Offers courses from top universities and companies, such as the "Machine Learning" course by Andrew Ng and the "Deep Learning Specialization" by deeplearning.ai.

2. **edX:**

- Provides courses from institutions like MIT and Harvard, including the "MicroMasters Program in Statistics and Data Science."

3. **Udacity:**

- Known for its "Nanodegree" programs, such as the "Machine Learning Engineer" and "AI for Healthcare" tracks.

4. **Khan Academy:**

- Offers foundational courses in mathematics, statistics, and programming.

Research Papers and Journals:

1. **arXiv:**

- A repository of preprint papers in various fields, including machine learning and artificial intelligence. It is an excellent resource for accessing the latest research.

2. **Google Scholar:**

- A search engine for scholarly articles and papers across a wide range of disciplines. It is useful for finding research papers and citations.

3. **Journal of Machine Learning Research (JMLR):**

- Publishes high-quality research articles in the field of machine learning. It is a valuable resource for keeping up with cutting-edge developments.

4. **Conference Proceedings:**

- Proceedings from conferences like NeurIPS, ICML, and CVPR provide access to the latest research and innovations in machine learning and AI.

Blogs and Websites:

1. **Towards Data Science:**

- A medium publication featuring articles on data science, machine learning, and AI. It is a great resource for tutorials, case studies, and industry insights.

2. **KDnuggets:**

- A leading site for data science, machine learning, and AI news, articles, and resources. It offers a wealth of information for practitioners at all levels.

3. **Distill:**

- A journal dedicated to clear and accessible explanations of machine learning research. It features visually engaging articles that make complex concepts easier to understand.

4. **Analytics Vidhya:**

- A platform offering tutorials, articles, and competitions in data science and machine learning. It is a great resource for learning new skills and staying updated with industry trends.

Communities and Forums:

1. **Reddit:**

- Subreddits like r/MachineLearning and r/DataScience are great for discussions, news, and resources. These communities offer a platform to engage with peers and experts.

2. **Stack Overflow:**

- A popular forum for asking and answering technical questions related to programming and machine learning. It is an invaluable resource for troubleshooting and learning from others.

3. **Kaggle:**
- A community platform for data science competitions, datasets, and notebooks. It offers opportunities to practice skills, collaborate with others, and gain recognition in the community.

4. **Data Science Stack Exchange:**
- A Q&A site for data science and machine learning practitioners. It provides a platform to seek advice and share knowledge with peers.

Index

Accuracy: 22, 30, 32-33, 39, 47, 49, 51, 75, 84, 93, 98, 112

Algorithm: 14, 21, 93, 98

Anomaly Detection: 4, 48, 70-71, 93, 98, 127

AutoML: 1, 4, 6, 9, 12, 56-58, 60, 78-79, 90, 93, 98, 124-126

Bias: 36, 93, 98

Bias-Variance Tradeoff: 98

Cross-Validation: 22, 93, 98

Data Preprocessing: 3, 27, 64, 68, 71, 74, 93, 98, 105, 108, 124-126

Deep Learning: 44, 84, 93, 96, 98, 102

Dimensionality Reduction: 20, 93, 98

Evaluation Metrics: 5, 22, 84, 94, 98, 113

Feature Engineering: 3, 20, 27, 43, 47, 57, 68, 71, 74, 94, 98, 106-107, 121, 125-128

Federated Learning: 4, 9, 12, 58, 78, 90, 94, 98

Hyperparameter Tuning: 3, 22-23, 30-31, 52, 94, 99, 125-126

K-Means Clustering: 84, 94, 99

L1 Regularization: 94, 99

L2 Regularization: 94, 99

Logistic Regression: 83, 94, 99

Machine Learning: 4, 9, 12, 56, 60, 90, 93-94, 96-97, 99

Model Deployment: 23, 56, 94, 99

Model Evaluation: 3, 17, 22, 32, 94, 99

Neural Network: 94, 99

Overfitting: 21, 24, 94-95, 99

Precision: 32-33, 84, 95, 99, 112

Principal Component Analysis: 20, 84, 93, 99

Recall: 32-33, 84, 95, 99, 112

Regression: 22, 30, 52, 83, 85, 94-95, 99

ROC-AUC: 22, 33, 84, 89, 94-95, 99, 112

Scalability: 3, 7, 14, 23, 34, 39, 42-43, 47, 51, 56, 58, 67, 89, 95, 99

Supervised Learning: 48, 83, 95, 99

Support Vector Machine: 95, 99

Unsupervised Learning: 84, 95, 99

XGBoost: 95, 99

Conclusion

The glossary of terms, additional resources, and index provided in this appendix serve as valuable tools for reinforcing your understanding of machine learning concepts and techniques. Use these resources to deepen your knowledge, stay updated with industry trends, and continue your journey in the exciting field of machine learning. With the right tools and resources at your disposal, you are well-equipped to succeed and make meaningful contributions to the world of ML and AI.

BONUS
Detailed Diagrams and Visual Aids

Industry Trends in ML Hiring Diagram: ML Hiring Trends

- **Purpose:** This diagram illustrates the most in-demand skills and roles in the ML job market
- **Key Components:**
- **Demand for Skills:** Visual representation of the increasing demand for specific skills such as deep learning, data engineering, and AI ethics.
- **Sector Growth:** Highlights sectors with the highest ML hiring growth, such as healthcare, finance, and technology.
- **How it Helps:** Provides insights into where to focus your learning and career efforts based on industry demand.

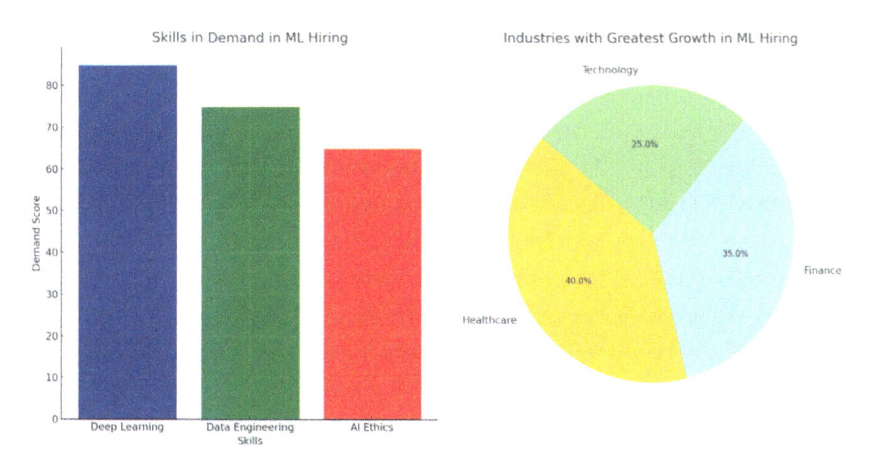

Here is the diagram illustrating the industry trends in ML hiring:

1. **Skills in Demand in ML Hiring:**

- Shows the growing demand for skills in areas such as deep learning, data engineering, and artificial intelligence ethics.

2. **Industries with Greatest Growth in ML Hiring:**

- Highlights the industries with the greatest growth in ML hiring, such as healthcare, finance, and technology.

CODE

```
import matplotlib.pyplot as plt
```

Data for skills in demand

```
skills = ['Deep Learning', 'Data Engineering', 'AI Ethics']
demand = [85, 75, 65] # Hypothetical demand scores
```

Data for industries with greatest growth in ML hiring

```
industries = ['Healthcare', 'Finance', 'Technology']
growth = [40, 35, 25] # Hypothetical growth percentages
fig, (ax1, ax2) = plt.subplots(1, 2, figsize=(14, 7))
```

Bar chart for skills in demand

```
ax1.bar(skills, demand, color=['blue', 'green', 'red'])
ax1.set_title('Skills in Demand in ML Hiring')
ax1.set_xlabel('Skills')
ax1.set_ylabel('Demand Score')
```

Pie chart for industries with greatest growth in ML hiring

```
ax2.pie(growth, labels=industries, autopct='%1.1f%%', startangle=140, colors=['gold', 'lightblue', 'lightgreen'])
ax2.set_title('Industries with Greatest Growth in ML Hiring')
plt.tight_layout()
plt.savefig("/mnt/data/ML_hiring_trends.png")
plt.show()
```

Overview of the ML Interview Process

Diagram: ML Interview Process Flowchart

- **Purpose:** Outlines the typical stages of an ML interview process from application to final offer.
- **Key Components:**
- **Resume Screening:** Initial stage where resumes are reviewed.
- **Technical Assessments:** Coding challenges and technical questions.
- **System Design Interviews:** Evaluation of system design skills.

- **Behavioral Interviews:** Assessment of soft skills and cultural fit.
- **How it Helps:** Helps candidates understand the steps involved and prepare accordingly for each stage.

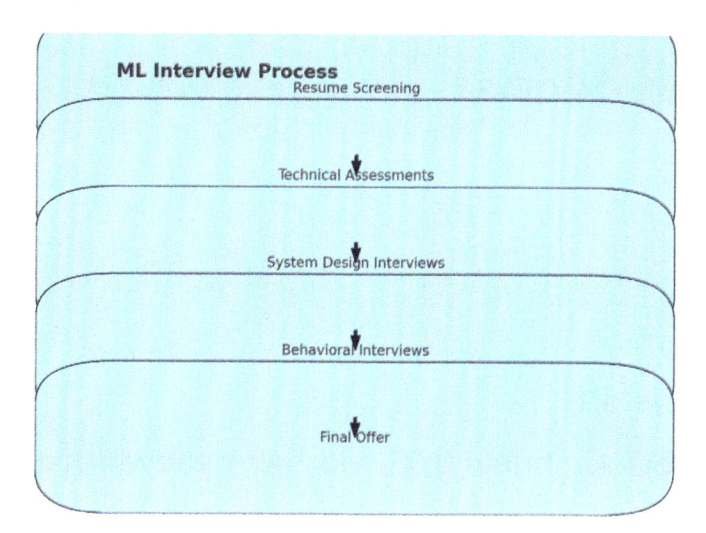

Here is the diagram outlining the overview of the ML interview process. The flowchart depicts the typical steps involved, from resume screening to the final offer.

1. **Resume Screening**: Initial stage where resumes are reviewed.
2. **Technical Assessments**: Coding challenges and technical questions.
3. **System Design Interviews**: Assessment of system design skills.
4. **Behavioral Interviews**: Assessment of soft skills and cultural fit.
5. **Final Offer**: Conclusion of the interview process.

This flowchart helps candidates understand the stages involved and prepare accordingly for each stage.

CODE

import matplotlib.pyplot as plt

import matplotlib.patches as mpatches

fig, ax = plt.subplots(figsize=(10, 6))

Create a flowchart using rectangles and arrows

flow_labels = ['Resume Screening', 'Technical Assessments', 'System Design Interviews', 'Behavioral Interviews', 'Final Offer']

rect_positions = [(0.1, 0.8), (0.1, 0.6), (0.1, 0.4), (0.1, 0.2), (0.1, 0.0)]

for i, (x, y) in enumerate(rect_positions):

rect = mpatches.FancyBboxPatch((x, y), 0.6, 0.15, boxstyle="round,pad=0.1", edgecolor='black', facecolor='lightblue') ax.add_patch(rect)

ax.text(x + 0.3, y + 0.075, flow_labels[i], ha='center', va='center', fontsize=12)

Add arrows

arrow_positions = [((0.4, 0.725), (0.4, 0.675)),

((0.4, 0.525), (0.4, 0.475)),

((0.4, 0.325), (0.4, 0.275)),

((0.4, 0.125), (0.4, 0.075))]

for start, end in arrow_positions:

ax.annotate('', xy=end, xytext=start,

arrowprops=dict(facecolor='black', shrink=0.05, width=2, headwidth=8))

ax.text(0.1, 0.9, 'ML Interview Process', fontsize=16, fontweight='bold')

ax.set_xlim(0, 1)

ax.set_ylim(-0.1, 1)

ax.axis('off')

plt.tight_layout()

plt.savefig("/mnt/data/ML_interview_process_flowchart.png")

plt.show()

Key Skills and Knowledge for ML Interviews

Diagram: Key Skills for ML Interviews

- **Purpose:** Highlights essential skills and knowledge areas for ML interviews.
- **Key Components:**
- **Technical Skills:** Programming, mathematics, data preprocessing, model selection.
- **Soft Skills:** Problem-solving, communication, teamwork.
- **How it Helps:** Guides candid

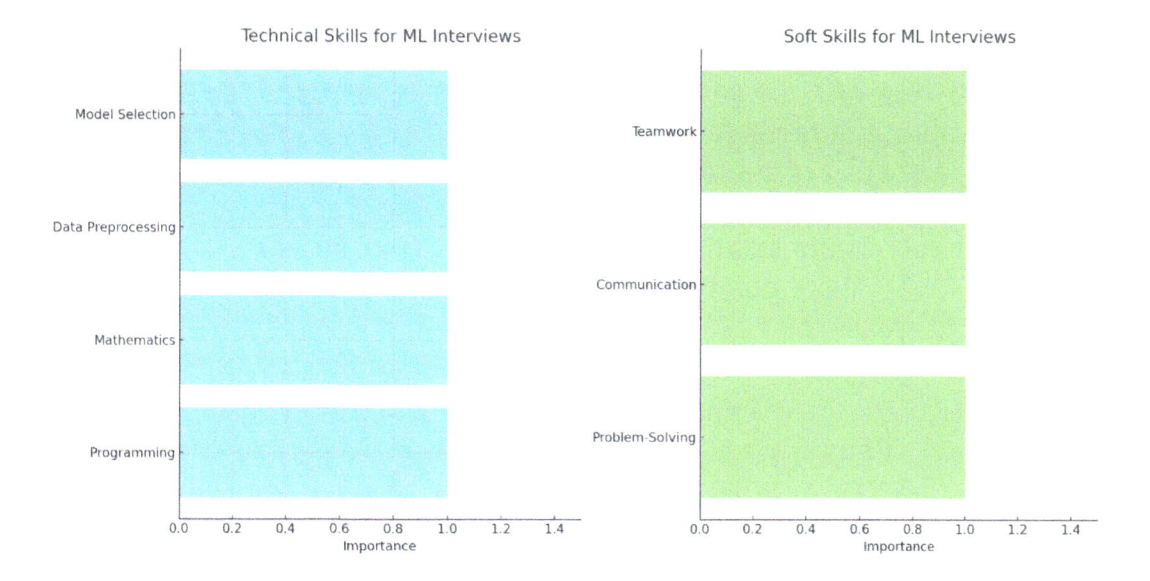

Here is the diagram highlighting the key skills and knowledge areas for ML interviews. The diagram is divided into two sections:

1. **Technical Skills for ML Interviews**:

- Programming
- Mathematics
- Data Preprocessing
- Model Selection

2. **Soft Skills for ML Interviews**:

- Problem-Solving
- Communication
- Teamwork

This diagram guides candidates on what areas to focus on while preparing for ML interviews, emphasizing both technical and soft skills.

CODE

```python
import matplotlib.pyplot as plt
```

Data for technical and soft skills

```python
technical_skills = ['Programming', 'Mathematics', 'Data
    Preprocessing', 'Model Selection']
soft_skills = ['Problem-Solving', 'Communication', 'Teamwork']
```

Positions for the bars

```python
technical_y = range(len(technical_skills))
soft_y = range(len(soft_skills))
fig, (ax1, ax2) = plt.subplots(1, 2, figsize=(14, 7))
```

Bar chart for technical skills

```
ax1.barh(technical_y, [1]*len(technical_skills), color='skyblue')
ax1.set_yticks(technical_y)
ax1.set_yticklabels(technical_skills)
ax1.set_xlim(0, 1.5)
ax1.set_title('Technical Skills for ML Interviews')
ax1.set_xlabel('Importance')
```

Bar chart for soft skills

```
ax2.barh(soft_y, [1]*len(soft_skills), color='lightgreen')
ax2.set_yticks(soft_y)
ax2.set_yticklabels(soft_skills)
ax2.set_xlim(0, 1.5)
ax2.set_title('Soft Skills for ML Interviews')
ax2.set_xlabel('Importance')
plt.tight_layout()
plt.savefig("/mnt/data/Key_Skills_for_ML_Interviews.png")
plt.show()
```

Data preprocessing techniques

Diagram: Data preprocessing pipeline

- **Purpose:** Shows the main steps of data preprocessing.
- **Key components:**
- **Data cleaning:** Removing noise and inconsistencies.
- **Normalization:** Scaling the data to a standard range.
- **Encoding:** Transforming categorical data into numerical form.
- **Feature Engineering:** Creating new features to improve model performance.

How it helps: Providing

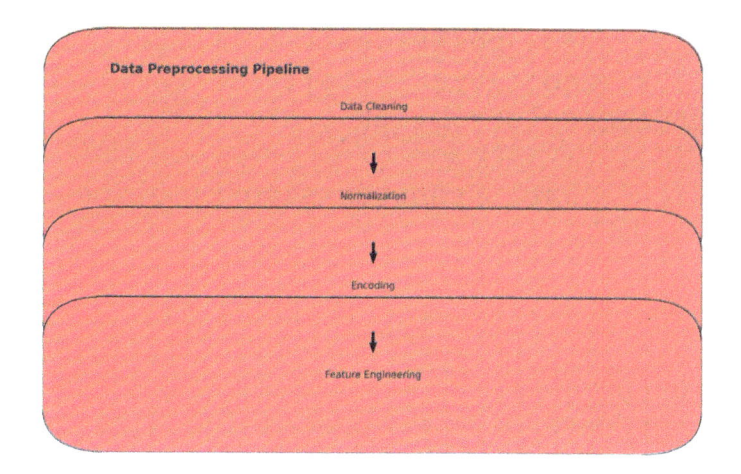

Here is the diagram illustrating the data preprocessing pipeline. The diagram shows the main steps involved in data preprocessing:

1. Data Cleaning: Removing noise and inconsistencies.
2. Normalization: Scaling the data to a standard range.
3. Encoding: Transforming categorical data into numerical form.
4. Feature Engineering: Creating new features to improve model performance.

This visual representation helps in understanding the sequential steps involved in preparing data for machine learning models, ensuring data quality and improving model performance

CODE

```python
import matplotlib.pyplot as plt
import matplotlib.patches as mpatches

fig, ax = plt.subplots(figsize=(12, 8))
```

Create a pipeline flowchart using rectangles and arrows

```python
pipeline_labels = ['Data Cleaning', 'Normalization', 'Encoding',
    'Feature Engineering']
rect_positions = [(0.1, 0.7), (0.1, 0.5), (0.1, 0.3), (0.1, 0.1)]
for i, (x, y) in enumerate(rect_positions):
rect = mpatches.FancyBboxPatch((x, y), 0.8, 0.15,
    boxstyle="round,pad=0.1", edgecolor='black',
    facecolor='lightcoral')
ax.add_patch(rect)
ax.text(x + 0.4, y + 0.075, pipeline_labels[i], ha='center',
    va='center', fontsize=12)
```

Add arrows

```python
arrow_positions = [((0.5, 0.675), (0.5, 0.625)),
((0.5, 0.475), (0.5, 0.425)),
```

```
            ((0.5, 0.275), (0.5, 0.225))]
for start, end in arrow_positions:
ax.annotate('', xy=end, xytext=start,
   arrowprops=dict(facecolor='black', shrink=0.05, width=2,
      headwidth=8))
ax.text(0.1, 0.85, 'Data Preprocessing Pipeline', fontsize=16,
   fontweight='bold')
ax.set_xlim(0, 1)
ax.set_ylim(0, 1)
ax.axis('off')
plt.tight_layout()
plt.savefig("/mnt/data/Data_Preprocessing_Pipeline.png")
plt.show()
```

Model selection process

Diagram: Model selection workflow.

- Purpose: Illustrates the process of selecting the appropriate ML model.
- Key Components:
- Problem understanding: Problem definition and requirements.
- Data characteristics: Evaluation of data to select suitable models.
- Model comparison: Comparison of different models using cross-validation and metrics.
- How it helps: Guides practitioners to make informed decisions when choosing models for their projects.

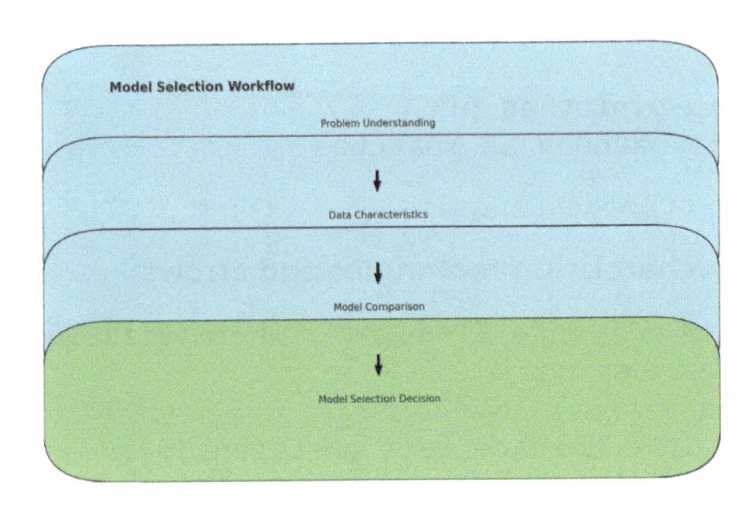

Here is the diagram illustrating the model selection workflow. The diagram shows the key steps involved in selecting the appropriate ML model:

1. **Problem Understanding**: Defining the problem and its requirements.
2. **Data Characteristics**: Evaluating the data to select suitable models.
3. **Model Comparison**: Comparing different models using cross-validation and metrics.
4. **Model Selection Decision**: Making an informed decision on the best model to use for the project.

This visual representation helps practitioners understand the sequential steps involved in choosing the right model for their projects.

code

```python
import matplotlib.pyplot as plt
import matplotlib.patches as mpatches

fig, ax = plt.subplots(figsize=(12, 8))
```

Create a workflow diagram using rectangles and arrows

```python
workflow_labels = ['Problem Understanding', 'Data Characteristics', 'Model Comparison']
rect_positions = [(0.1, 0.7), (0.1, 0.5), (0.1, 0.3)]
for i, (x, y) in enumerate(rect_positions):
    rect = mpatches.FancyBboxPatch((x, y), 0.8, 0.15,
        boxstyle="round,pad=0.1", edgecolor='black',
        facecolor='lightblue')
    ax.add_patch(rect)
    ax.text(x + 0.4, y + 0.075, workflow_labels[i], ha='center',
        va='center', fontsize=12)
```

Add arrows

```python
arrow_positions = [((0.5, 0.675), (0.5, 0.625)),
((0.5, 0.475), (0.5, 0.425))]
for start, end in arrow_positions:
    ax.annotate('', xy=end, xytext=start,
    arrowprops=dict(facecolor='black', shrink=0.05, width=2,
        headwidth=8))
```

Add final decision box

```python
final_rect = mpatches.FancyBboxPatch((0.1, 0.1), 0.8,
    0.15, boxstyle="round,pad=0.1", edgecolor='black',
    facecolor='lightgreen')
ax.add_patch(final_rect)
ax.text(0.5, 0.175, 'Model Selection Decision', ha='center',
    va='center', fontsize=12)
```

Add final arrow

```python
ax.annotate('', xy=(0.5, 0.225), xytext=(0.5, 0.275),
arrowprops=dict(facecolor='black', shrink=0.05, width=2,
    headwidth=8))
ax.text(0.1, 0.85, 'Model Selection Workflow', fontsize=16,
    fontweight='bold')
ax.set_xlim(0, 1)
ax.set_ylim(0, 1)
```

```
ax.axis('off')
plt.tight_layout()
plt.savefig("/mnt/data/Model_Selection_Workflow.png")
plt.show()
create this diagram for me
```

Methods of adjusting hyperparameters

Diagram: Hyperparameter adjustment techniques

- **Purpose:** Illustrates the various techniques for adjusting hyperparameters.
- **Key Components:**
- **Grid search:** Exhaustive search on specified parameter values.
- **Random search:** Random sampling of parameter values.
- **Bayesian optimization:** Use of probabilistic models to guide the search.
- **How it is useful:** Helps to understand and apply different methods to optimize model performance.

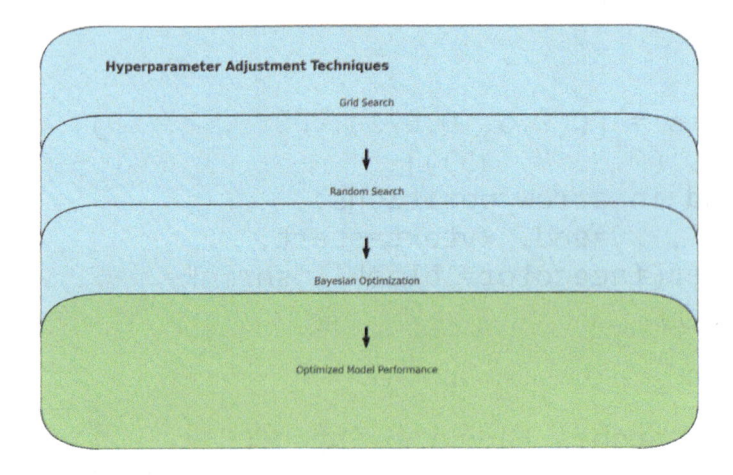

Here is the diagram illustrating hyperparameter adjustment techniques. The diagram shows the key methods for adjusting hyperparameters:

1. **Grid Search**: Exhaustive search on specified parameter values.
2. **Random Search**: Random sampling of parameter values.
3. **Bayesian Optimization**: Use of probabilistic models to guide the search.
4. **Optimized Model Performance**: The outcome of applying these techniques.

This visual representation helps to understand and apply different methods to optimize model performance.

CODE

```
import matplotlib.pyplot as plt
```

```python
import matplotlib.patches as mpatches
fig, ax = plt.subplots(figsize=(12, 8))
```
Create a diagram using rectangles and arrows
```python
methods_labels = ['Grid Search', 'Random Search', 'Bayesian Optimization']
rect_positions = [(0.1, 0.7), (0.1, 0.5), (0.1, 0.3)]
for i, (x, y) in enumerate(rect_positions):
rect = mpatches.FancyBboxPatch((x, y), 0.8, 0.15,
    boxstyle="round,pad=0.1", edgecolor='black',
    facecolor='lightblue')
ax.add_patch(rect)
ax.text(x + 0.4, y + 0.075, methods_labels[i], ha='center',
    va='center', fontsize=12)
```
Add arrows
```python
arrow_positions = [((0.5, 0.675), (0.5, 0.625)),
((0.5, 0.475), (0.5, 0.425)),
((0.5, 0.275), (0.5, 0.225))]
for start, end in arrow_positions:
ax.annotate('', xy=end, xytext=start,
arrowprops=dict(facecolor='black', shrink=0.05, width=2,
    headwidth=8))
```
Add final decision box
```python
final_rect = mpatches.FancyBboxPatch((0.1, 0.1), 0.8,
    0.15, boxstyle="round,pad=0.1", edgecolor='black',
    facecolor='lightgreen')
ax.add_patch(final_rect)
ax.text(0.5, 0.175, 'Optimized Model Performance', ha='center',
    va='center', fontsize=12)
```
Add final arrow
```python
ax.annotate('', xy=(0.5, 0.225), xytext=(0.5, 0.275),
arrowprops=dict(facecolor='black', shrink=0.05, width=2,
    headwidth=8))
ax.text(0.1, 0.85, 'Hyperparameter Adjustment Techniques',
    fontsize=16, fontweight='bold')
ax.set_xlim(0, 1)
ax.set_ylim(0, 1)
ax.axis('off')
plt.tight_layout()
plt.savefig("/mnt/data/Hyperparameter_Adjustment_Techniques.png")
plt.show()
```

Evaluation metrics explained

Diagram: Evaluation metrics for classification.

- **Purpose:** Provides a visual explanation of common evaluation metrics for classification models.
- **Key Components:**
- **Accuracy:** Ratio of instances predicted correctly.
- **Accuracy:** Ratio of true and positive predictions to total positive predictions.
- **Recall:** Ratio of true positive predictions to total true positive predictions.
- **F1 score:** harmonic mean of accuracy and recall.
- **ROC-AUC:** Area under the ROC curve.
- **How useful:** Helps select and interpret appropriate metrics to evaluate model performance.

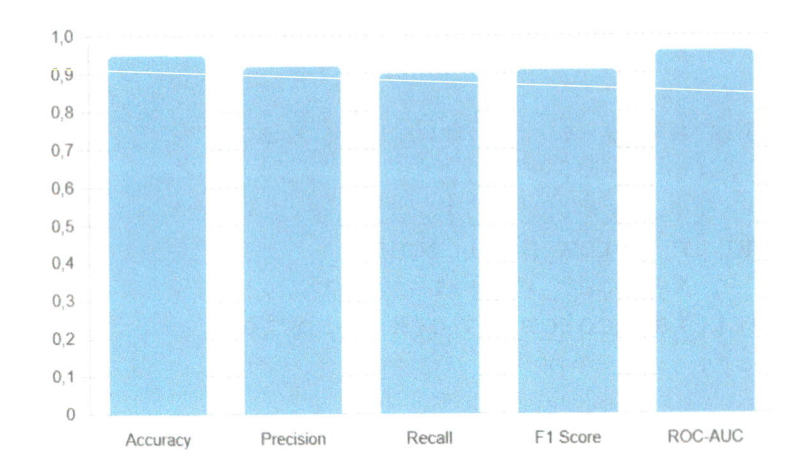

Here is the diagram explaining the evaluation metrics for classification models. The bar chart provides a visual explanation of common evaluation metrics:

1. **Accuracy**: Ratio of instances predicted correctly.
2. **Precision**: Ratio of true positive predictions to total positive predictions.
3. **Recall**: Ratio of true positive predictions to total true positives.
4. **F1 Score**: Harmonic mean of precision and recall.
5. **ROC-AUC**: Area under the ROC curve.

This visual representation helps in selecting and interpreting appropriate metrics to evaluate model performance.

CODE

```python
import matplotlib.pyplot as plt
import numpy as np
```

Data for evaluation metrics

```python
metrics = ['Accuracy', 'Precision', 'Recall', 'F1 Score', 'ROC-AUC']
```

```python
values = [0.95, 0.92, 0.90, 0.91, 0.96] # Hypothetical values for
    illustration
fig, ax = plt.subplots(figsize=(12, 8))
```

Bar chart for evaluation metrics

```python
bars = ax.bar(metrics, values, color='skyblue')
```

Add value labels on the bars

```python
for bar in bars:
height = bar.get_height()
ax.text(bar.get_x() + bar.get_width() / 2, height - 0.05,
    f'{height:.2f}', ha='center', va='bottom', fontsize=12)
ax.set_ylim(0, 1.1)
ax.set_title('Evaluation Metrics for Classification', fontsize=16,
    fontweight='bold')
ax.set_ylabel('Score')
ax.set_xlabel('Metrics')
plt.tight_layout()
plt.savefig("/mnt/data/Evaluation_Metrics_for_Classification.png")
plt.show()
```

Scaling strategies and performance optimization

Diagram: Scaling strategies for ML models

- **Purpose:** Outlines strategies for scaling ML models.
- **Key Components:**
- **Parallel processing:** Distribution of tasks across multiple processors.
- **Distributed processing:** Use of a computer network for large-scale processing.
- **Model optimization**: Techniques such as quantization and pruning.
- **How it helps:** Provides methods to ensure that models can handle large data sets and improve performance.

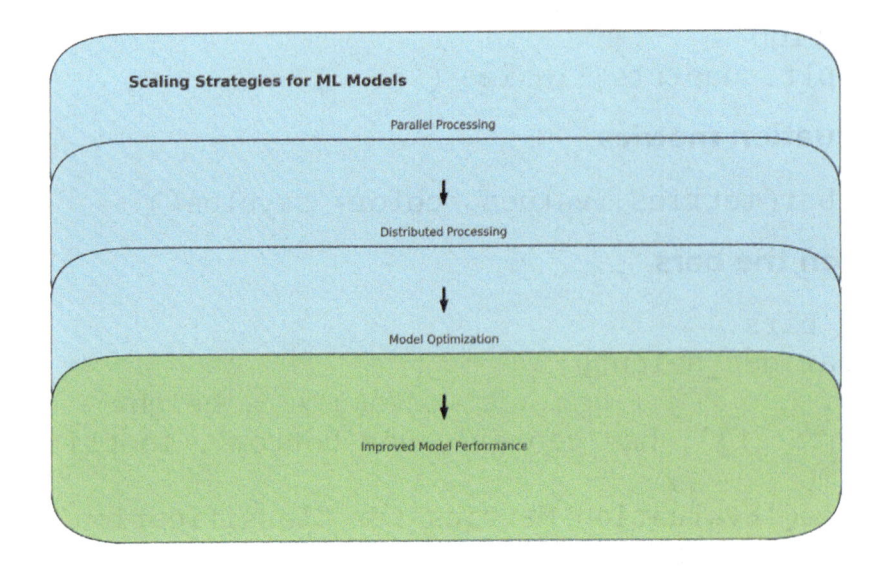

Here is the diagram illustrating the scaling strategies for ML models. The diagram outlines the key components involved in scaling and optimizing performance:

1. **Parallel Processing**: Distribution of tasks across multiple processors.
2. **Distributed Processing**: Use of a computer network for large-scale processing.
3. **Model Optimization**: Techniques such as quantization and pruning.
4. **Improved Model Performance**: The outcome of applying these strategies.

This visual representation provides methods to ensure that models can handle large datasets and improve performance.

CODE

```python
import matplotlib.pyplot as plt
import matplotlib.patches as mpatches

fig, ax = plt.subplots(figsize=(12, 8))
```

Create a diagram using rectangles and arrows

```python
scaling_labels = ['Parallel Processing', 'Distributed Processing',
    'Model Optimization']
rect_positions = [(0.1, 0.7), (0.1, 0.5), (0.1, 0.3)]
for i, (x, y) in enumerate(rect_positions):
rect = mpatches.FancyBboxPatch((x, y), 0.8, 0.15,
    boxstyle="round,pad=0.1", edgecolor='black',
    facecolor='lightblue')
ax.add_patch(rect)
ax.text(x + 0.4, y + 0.075, scaling_labels[i], ha='center',
    va='center', fontsize=12)
```

Add arrows

```python
    arrow_positions = [((0.5, 0.675), (0.5, 0.625)),
                       ((0.5, 0.475), (0.5, 0.425)),
                       ((0.5, 0.275), (0.5, 0.225))]
    for start, end in arrow_positions:
        ax.annotate('', xy=end, xytext=start,
            arrowprops=dict(facecolor='black', shrink=0.05, width=2,
                headwidth=8))
```

Add final decision box

```python
    final_rect = mpatches.FancyBboxPatch((0.1, 0.1), 0.8,
        0.15, boxstyle="round,pad=0.1", edgecolor='black',
        facecolor='lightgreen')
    ax.add_patch(final_rect)
    ax.text(0.5, 0.175, 'Improved Model Performance', ha='center',
        va='center', fontsize=12)
```

Add final arrow

```python
    ax.annotate('', xy=(0.5, 0.225), xytext=(0.5, 0.275),
        arrowprops=dict(facecolor='black', shrink=0.05, width=2,
            headwidth=8))
    ax.text(0.1, 0.85, 'Scaling Strategies for ML Models', fontsize=16,
        fontweight='bold')
    ax.set_xlim(0, 1)
    ax.set_ylim(0, 1)
    ax.axis('off')
    plt.tight_layout()
    plt.savefig("/mnt/data/Scaling_Strategies_for_ML_Models.png")
    plt.show()
```

Ethical and equity frameworks

Diagram: AI ethical framework

- **Purpose:** Illustrates a framework for ensuring ethical and fair AI practices.
- **Key Components:**
- **Fairness:** Ensuring unbiased model predictions.
- **Transparency:** Making model decisions understandable.
- **Accountability:** Accountability for model results.
- **Privacy:** Protection of user data.
- **How it helps:** Guide practitioners in building ethical AI systems and managing bias.

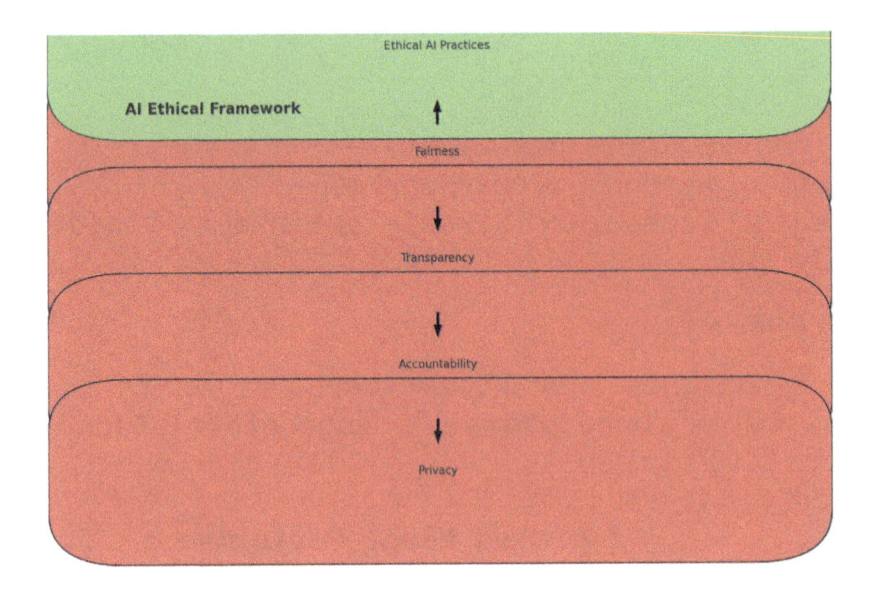

Here is the diagram illustrating the AI ethical framework. The diagram outlines the key components involved in ensuring ethical and fair AI practices:

1. **Fairness**: Ensuring unbiased model predictions.
2. **Transparency**: Making model decisions understandable.
3. **Accountability**: Responsibility for model results.
4. **Privacy**: Protection of user data.
5. **Ethical AI Practices**: The outcome of applying these principles.

This visual representation guides practitioners in building ethical AI systems and managing bias.

CODE

```python
import matplotlib.pyplot as plt
import matplotlib.patches as mpatches

fig, ax = plt.subplots(figsize=(12, 8))
```

Create a diagram using rectangles and arrows

```python
framework_labels = ['Fairness', 'Transparency', 'Accountability',
    'Privacy']
rect_positions = [(0.1, 0.7), (0.1, 0.5), (0.1, 0.3), (0.1, 0.1)]
for i, (x, y) in enumerate(rect_positions):
rect = mpatches.FancyBboxPatch((x, y), 0.8, 0.15,
    boxstyle="round,pad=0.1", edgecolor='black',
    facecolor='lightcoral')
ax.add_patch(rect)
ax.text(x + 0.4, y + 0.075, framework_labels[i], ha='center',
    va='center', fontsize=12)
```

Add arrows

```python
arrow_positions = [((0.5, 0.675), (0.5, 0.625)),
                   ((0.5, 0.475), (0.5, 0.425)),
                   ((0.5, 0.275), (0.5, 0.225))]
for start, end in arrow_positions:
    ax.annotate('', xy=end, xytext=start,
        arrowprops=dict(facecolor='black', shrink=0.05, width=2,
            headwidth=8))
```

Add final decision box

```python
final_rect = mpatches.FancyBboxPatch((0.1, 0.9), 0.8,
    0.15, boxstyle="round,pad=0.1", edgecolor='black',
    facecolor='lightgreen')
ax.add_patch(final_rect)
ax.text(0.5, 0.975, 'Ethical AI Practices', ha='center',
    va='center', fontsize=12)
```

Add final arrow

```python
ax.annotate('', xy=(0.5, 0.875), xytext=(0.5, 0.825),
    arrowprops=dict(facecolor='black', shrink=0.05, width=2,
        headwidth=8))
ax.text(0.1, 0.85, 'AI Ethical Framework', fontsize=16,
    fontweight='bold')
ax.set_xlim(0, 1)
ax.set_ylim(0, 1)
ax.axis('off')
plt.tight_layout()
plt.savefig("/mnt/data/AI_Ethical_Framework.png")
plt.show()
```

Case study diagrams

Architecture of the visual search system

Diagram: Architecture of the visual search system

- **Purpose:** Shows the components of a visual search system.
- **Key components:**
- **Data ingestion:** Collection of images.
- **Feature Extraction:** Processing images to extract features.
- **Similarity Matching:** Comparison of features to find similar items.
- **User Interface:** Displaying results to users.

- **How it helps:** Provides an outline for building a visual search system.

Workflow for real-time content recommendation.

Diagram: Workflow for real-time content recommendation.

- **Purpose:** Illustrates the process of providing real-time content recommendation.
- **Key components:**
- **Data collection:** Collection of user interaction data.
- **Feature extraction:** Creation of features from interactions.
- **Model training:** Training of recommendation models.
- **Service recommendations:** Providing recommendations to users.
- **How it helps:** Explain the end-to-end process of creating a recommendation engine.

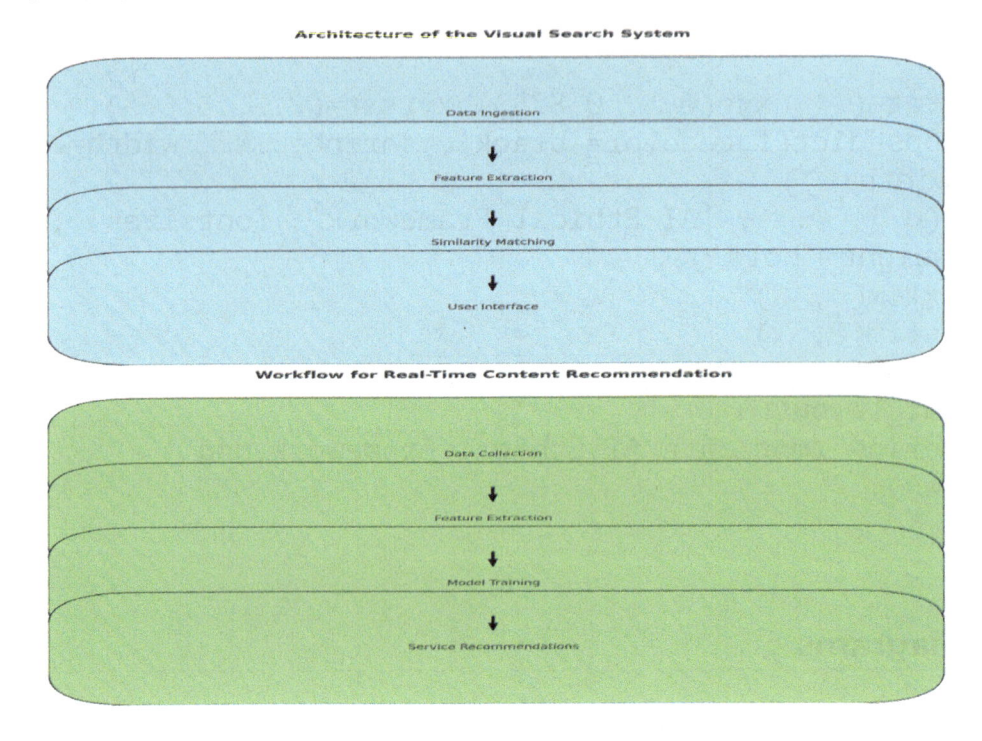

Architecture of the Visual Search System

Data Ingestion
↓
Feature Extraction
↓
Similarity Matching
↓
User Interface

Workflow for Real-Time Content Recommendation

Data Collection
↓
Feature Extraction
↓
Model Training
↓
Service Recommendations

Here are the diagrams for the case studies:

Architecture of the Visual Search System

1. **Data Ingestion**: Collection of images.
2. **Feature Extraction**: Processing images to extract features.
3. **Similarity Matching**: Comparison of features to find similar items.
4. **User Interface**: Displaying results to users.

Workflow for Real-Time Content Recommendation

1. **Data Collection**: Collection of user interaction data.
2. **Feature Extraction**: Creation of features from interactions.
3. **Model Training**: Training of recommendation models.
4. **Service Recommendations**: Providing recommendations to users.

These diagrams provide an outline for building a visual search system and explain the end-to-end process of creating a recommendation engine.

CODE

```python
import matplotlib.pyplot as plt
import matplotlib.patches as mpatches

fig, (ax1, ax2) = plt.subplots(2, 1, figsize=(12, 16))
```

Architecture of the Visual Search System

```python
visual_search_labels = ['Data Ingestion', 'Feature Extraction',
    'Similarity Matching', 'User Interface']
rect_positions_vss = [(0.1, 0.7), (0.1, 0.5), (0.1, 0.3), (0.1,
    0.1)]
for i, (x, y) in enumerate(rect_positions_vss):
rect = mpatches.FancyBboxPatch((x, y), 0.8, 0.15,
    boxstyle="round,pad=0.1", edgecolor='black',
    facecolor='lightblue')
ax1.add_patch(rect)
ax1.text(x + 0.4, y + 0.075, visual_search_labels[i], ha='center',
    va='center', fontsize=12)
```

Add arrows

```python
arrow_positions_vss = [((0.5, 0.675), (0.5, 0.625)),
((0.5, 0.475), (0.5, 0.425)),
((0.5, 0.275), (0.5, 0.225))]
for start, end in arrow_positions_vss:
ax1.annotate('', xy=end, xytext=start,
arrowprops=dict(facecolor='black', shrink=0.05, width=2,
    headwidth=8))
ax1.set_title('Architecture of the Visual Search System',
    fontsize=16, fontweight='bold')
ax1.axis('off')
```

Workflow for Real-Time Content Recommendation

```python
recommendation_labels = ['Data Collection', 'Feature Extraction',
    'Model Training', 'Service Recommendations']
```

```python
rect_positions_rc = [(0.1, 0.7), (0.1, 0.5), (0.1, 0.3), (0.1,
    0.1)]
for i, (x, y) in enumerate(rect_positions_rc):
rect = mpatches.FancyBboxPatch((x, y), 0.8, 0.15,
    boxstyle="round,pad=0.1", edgecolor='black',
    facecolor='lightgreen')
ax2.add_patch(rect)
ax2.text(x + 0.4, y + 0.075, recommendation_labels[i], ha='center',
    va='center', fontsize=12)
```

Add arrows

```python
arrow_positions_rc = [((0.5, 0.675), (0.5, 0.625)),
((0.5, 0.475), (0.5, 0.425)),
((0.5, 0.275), (0.5, 0.225))]
for start, end in arrow_positions_rc:
ax2.annotate('', xy=end, xytext=start,
arrowprops=dict(facecolor='black', shrink=0.05, width=2,
    headwidth=8))
ax2.set_title('Workflow for Real-Time Content Recommendation',
    fontsize=16, fontweight='bold')
ax2.axis('off')
plt.tight_layout()
plt.savefig("/mnt/data/Case_Study_Diagrams.png")
plt.show()
```

Designing an advanced fraud detection system

Diagram: Design of a fraud detection system

- **Purpose:** Illustrates the design of a fraud detection system.
- **Key components:**
- **Transaction monitoring:** Collection of transaction data.
- **Feature engineering:** Creation of features indicative of fraud.
- **Model** training: Training of models to detect anomalies.
- **Alert generation:** Generation of alerts for suspected fraud.
- **How it helps:** Provides a framework for implementing fraud detection.

Design of a Fraud Detection System

[Transaction Monitoring]
↓
[Feature Engineering]
↓
[Model Training]
↓
[Alert Generation]

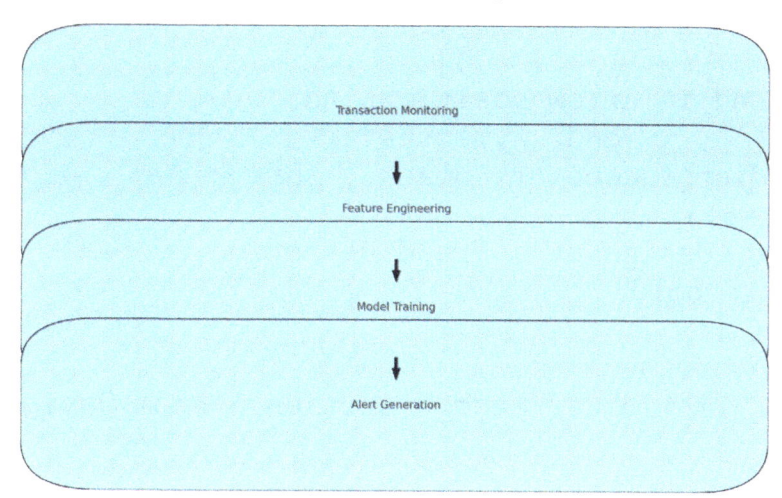

Here is the diagram illustrating the design of a fraud detection system. The diagram outlines the key components involved:

1. **Transaction Monitoring**: Collection of transaction data.
2. **Feature Engineering**: Creation of features indicative of fraud.
3. **Model Training**: Training of models to detect anomalies.
4. **Alert Generation**: Generation of alerts for suspected fraud.

This visual representation provides a framework for implementing a fraud detection system.

CODE

```python
import matplotlib.pyplot as plt
import matplotlib.patches as mpatches

    fig, ax = plt.subplots(figsize=(12, 8))
```

Create a diagram using rectangles and arrows

```python
    fraud_detection_labels = ['Transaction Monitoring', 'Feature
       Engineering', 'Model Training', 'Alert Generation']
    rect_positions_fd = [(0.1, 0.7), (0.1, 0.5), (0.1, 0.3), (0.1,
       0.1)]
    for i, (x, y) in enumerate(rect_positions_fd):
    rect = mpatches.FancyBboxPatch((x, y), 0.8, 0.15,
       boxstyle="round,pad=0.1", edgecolor='black',
       facecolor='lightblue')
    ax.add_patch(rect)
    ax.text(x + 0.4, y + 0.075, fraud_detection_labels[i], ha='center',
       va='center', fontsize=12)
```

Add arrows

```python
arrow_positions_fd = [((0.5, 0.675), (0.5, 0.625)),
((0.5, 0.475), (0.5, 0.425)),
((0.5, 0.275), (0.5, 0.225))]
for start, end in arrow_positions_fd:
ax.annotate('', xy=end, xytext=start,
arrowprops=dict(facecolor='black', shrink=0.05, width=2,
  headwidth=8))
ax.set_title('Design of a Fraud Detection System', fontsize=16,
  fontweight='bold')
ax.axis('off')
plt.tight_layout()
plt.savefig("/mnt/data/Fraud_Detection_System_Design.png")
plt.show()
```

Custom health prediction pipeline

Diagram: Health prediction pipeline

- **Purpose:** Shows the steps in building a personalized health prediction system.
- **Key components:**
- **Data integration:** Combination of EHR and wearable data.
- **Preprocessing:** Data cleaning and normalization.
- **Model** training: Training of health prediction models.
- **Deployment:** Use of models to provide health recommendations.
- **How it helps:** Guide the development of health prediction systems.

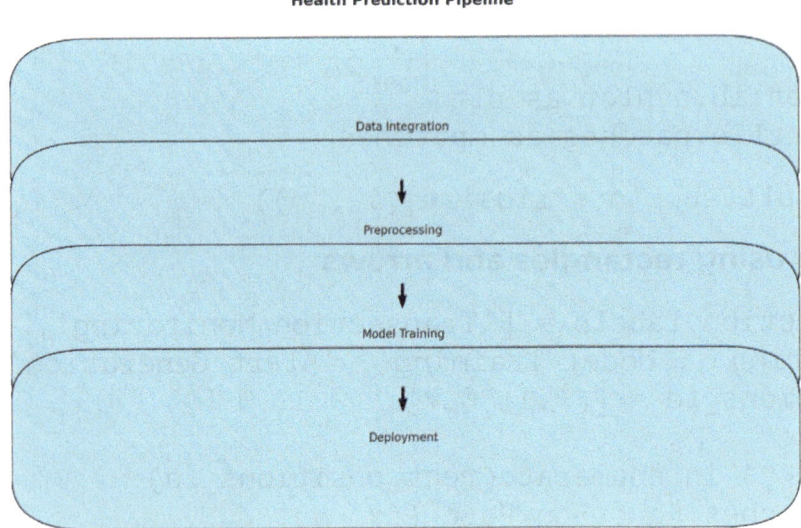

Health Prediction Pipeline

- Data Integration
- Preprocessing
- Model Training
- Deployment

Here is the diagram illustrating the health prediction pipeline. The diagram outlines the key components involved:

1. **Data Integration**: Combination of EHR and wearable data.
2. **Preprocessing**: Data cleaning and normalization.
3. **Model Training**: Training of health prediction models.

4. **Deployment**: Use of models to provide health recommendations.

This visual representation guides the development of personalized health prediction systems.

CODE

```python
import matplotlib.pyplot as plt
import matplotlib.patches as mpatches

fig, ax = plt.subplots(figsize=(12, 8))
```

Create a diagram using rectangles and arrows

```python
health_prediction_labels = ['Data Integration', 'Preprocessing',
    'Model Training', 'Deployment']
rect_positions_hp = [(0.1, 0.7), (0.1, 0.5), (0.1, 0.3), (0.1,
    0.1)]
for i, (x, y) in enumerate(rect_positions_hp):
rect = mpatches.FancyBboxPatch((x, y), 0.8, 0.15,
    boxstyle="round,pad=0.1", edgecolor='black',
    facecolor='lightblue')
ax.add_patch(rect)
ax.text(x + 0.4, y + 0.075, health_prediction_labels[i],
    ha='center', va='center', fontsize=12)
```

Add arrows

```python
arrow_positions_hp = [((0.5, 0.675), (0.5, 0.625)),
((0.5, 0.475), (0.5, 0.425)),
((0.5, 0.275), (0.5, 0.225))]
for start, end in arrow_positions_hp:
ax.annotate('', xy=end, xytext=start,
arrowprops=dict(facecolor='black', shrink=0.05, width=2,
    headwidth=8))
ax.set_title('Health Prediction Pipeline', fontsize=16,
    fontweight='bold')
ax.axis('off')
plt.tight_layout()
plt.savefig("/mnt/data/Health_Prediction_Pipeline.png")
plt.show()
```

Diagrams of Advanced ML Systems

Implementation of Artificial Intelligence on Edges

Diagram: Edge AI Implementation

- **Purpose:** Illustrates the implementation of AI on edge devices.
- **Key Components:**
- **Data Collection:** Gathering data at the edge.
- **On-Device Processing:** Processing data locally.
- **Cloud Integration:** Syncing data with cloud systems.
- **How it Helps:** Explains how to implement AI solutions that run on edge devices.

AutoML Workflow

Diagram: AutoML Workflow

- **Purpose:** Outlines the steps in an AutoML process.
- **Key Components:**
- **Data Preprocessing:** Automating data preparation.

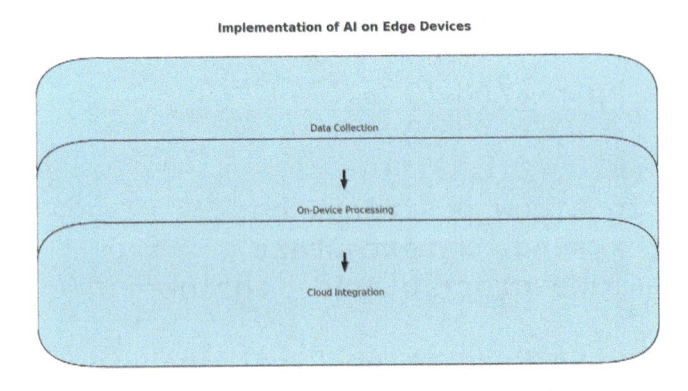

Implementation of AI on Edge Devices

Data Collection → On-Device Processing → Cloud Integration

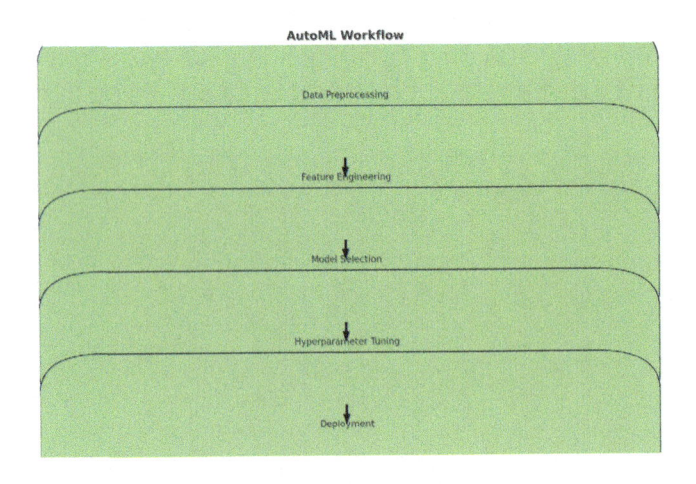

AutoML Workflow

Data Preprocessing → Feature Engineering → Model Selection → Hyperparameter Tuning → Deployment

Here are the diagrams illustrating the implementation of artificial intelligence on edge devices and the AutoML workflow:

Implementation of AI on Edge Devices

1. **Data Collection**: Data collection at the edge.
2. **On-Device Processing**: Local data processing.
3. **Cloud Integration**: Synchronizing data with cloud systems.

This visual representation explains how to implement AI solutions that work on edge devices.

AutoML Workflow

1. **Data Preprocessing**: Automating data preparation.
2. **Feature Engineering**: Creating features automatically.
3. **Model Selection**: Automatically selecting the best model.
4. **Hyperparameter Tuning**: Tuning model parameters.
5. **Deployment**: Deploying the optimized model.

This visual representation outlines the steps in an AutoML process.

CODE

```python
import matplotlib.pyplot as plt
import matplotlib.patches as mpatches

fig, (ax1, ax2) = plt.subplots(2, 1, figsize=(12, 16))
```

Implementation of AI on Edge Devices

```python
edge_ai_labels = ['Data Collection', 'On-Device Processing', 'Cloud
   Integration']
rect_positions_eai = [(0.1, 0.7), (0.1, 0.5), (0.1, 0.3)]
for i, (x, y) in enumerate(rect_positions_eai):
rect = mpatches.FancyBboxPatch((x, y), 0.8, 0.15,
   boxstyle="round,pad=0.1", edgecolor='black',
   facecolor='lightblue')
ax1.add_patch(rect)
ax1.text(x + 0.4, y + 0.075, edge_ai_labels[i], ha='center',
   va='center', fontsize=12)
```

Add arrows

```python
arrow_positions_eai = [((0.5, 0.675), (0.5, 0.625)),
  ((0.5, 0.475), (0.5, 0.425))]
for start, end in arrow_positions_eai:
ax1.annotate('', xy=end, xytext=start,
  arrowprops=dict(facecolor='black', shrink=0.05, width=2,
    headwidth=8))
ax1.set_title('Implementation of AI on Edge Devices', fontsize=16,
    fontweight='bold')
ax1.axis('off')
```

AutoML Workflow

```python
automl_labels = ['Data Preprocessing', 'Feature Engineering',
    'Model Selection', 'Hyperparameter Tuning', 'Deployment']
rect_positions_automl = [(0.1, 0.8), (0.1, 0.6), (0.1, 0.4), (0.1,
    0.2), (0.1, 0.0)]
for i, (x, y) in enumerate(rect_positions_automl):
rect = mpatches.FancyBboxPatch((x, y), 0.8, 0.15,
    boxstyle="round,pad=0.1", edgecolor='black',
    facecolor='lightgreen')
ax2.add_patch(rect)
ax2.text(x + 0.4, y + 0.075, automl_labels[i], ha='center',
    va='center', fontsize=12)
```

Add arrows

```python
arrow_positions_automl = [((0.5, 0.725), (0.5, 0.675)),
  ((0.5, 0.525), (0.5, 0.475)),
  ((0.5, 0.325), (0.5, 0.275)),
  ((0.5, 0.125), (0.5, 0.075))]
for start, end in arrow_positions_automl:
ax2.annotate('', xy=end, xytext=start,
  arrowprops=dict(facecolor='black', shrink=0.05, width=2,
    headwidth=8))
ax2.set_title('AutoML Workflow', fontsize=16, fontweight='bold')
ax2.axis('off')
plt.tight_layout()
plt.savefig("/mnt/data/Advanced_ML_Systems_Diagrams.png")
plt.show()
```

Practical Exercise Solutions Visuals:

1. **Designing a Social Media Monitoring System**

Visual Components:

- **Data Collection:** Diagram showing data sources such as social media platforms, APIs, and data storage.
- **Feature Engineering:** Illustration of text preprocessing, sentiment analysis, and feature extraction.
- **Model Training:** Flowchart of training the model with labeled data.
- **Deployment:** Overview of how the model is deployed to monitor social media in real-time.

2. **Building a Scalable Recommendation Engine for E-Commerce**

Visual Components:

- **Data Collection:** Diagram showing data from user interactions, product catalog, and purchase history.
- **Feature Engineering:** Illustration of collaborative filtering, content-based filtering, and hybrid methods.
- **Model Training:** Flowchart of training recommendation models.
- **Serving Recommendations:** Overview of real-time recommendation delivery to users.

3. **Developing a Real-Time Anomaly Detection System**

Visual Components:

- **Data Collection:** Diagram of data sources, such as sensors, logs, and transaction data.
- **Feature Engineering:** Illustration of statistical methods, moving averages, and anomaly scores.
- **Model Training:** Flowchart showing supervised and unsupervised anomaly detection techniques.
- **Alert Generation:** Overview of the process for real-time anomaly detection and alert systems.

4. **Creating a Predictive Maintenance System**

Visual Components:

- **Data Collection:** Diagram showing data from machinery, IoT devices, and historical maintenance records.
- **Feature Engineering:** Illustration of extracting features like usage patterns, wear and tear, and environmental conditions.
- **Model Training:** Flowchart of training models for predicting maintenance needs.
- **Deployment:** Overview of integrating the predictive model into maintenance scheduling systems.

Let's start with creating one of these diagrams as an example:

Designing a Social Media Monitoring System

Data Collection:

- **Diagram showing data sources such as social media platforms, APIs, and data storage.**

Feature Engineering:

- **Illustration of text preprocessing, sentiment analysis, and feature extraction.**

Model Training:

- **Flowchart of training the model with labeled data.**

Deployment:

- **Overview of how the model is deployed to monitor social media in real-time.**

Let's create the first diagram for "Designing a Social Media Monitoring System."

Designing a Social Media Monitoring System

Designing a Social Media Monitoring System

- Data Collection
  - ↓
- Feature Engineering
  - ↓
- Model Training
  - ↓
- Deployment

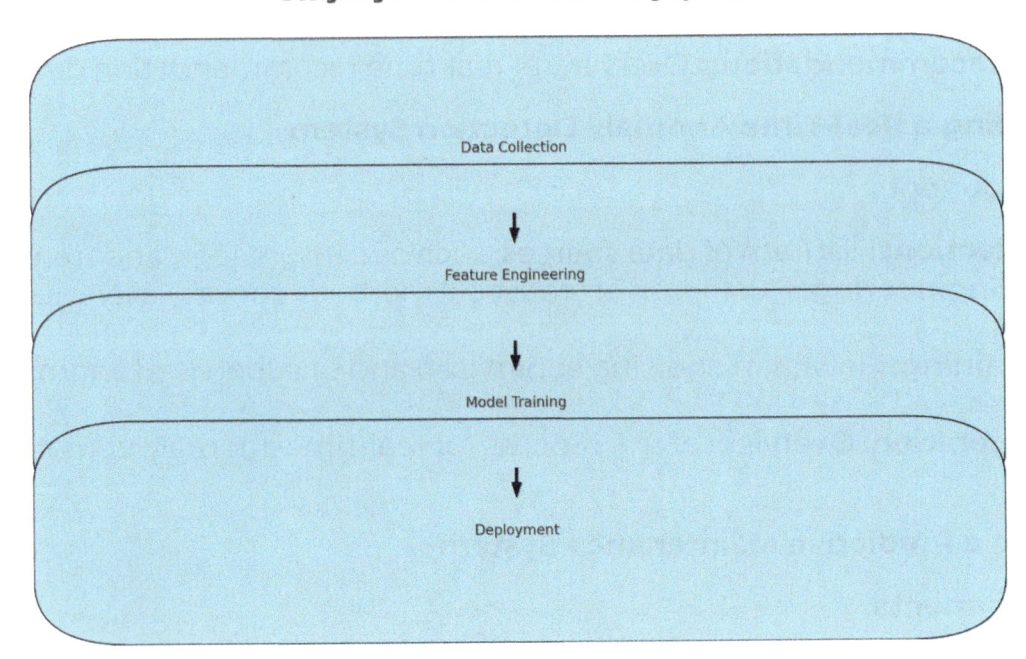

Here is the diagram for "Designing a Social Media Monitoring System". It outlines the key components involved:

1. **Data Collection:** Collection of data from social media platforms, APIs, and data storage.
2. **Feature Engineering:** Text preprocessing, sentiment analysis, and feature extraction.
3. **Model Training:** Training the model with labeled data.

4. **Deployment:** Deploying the model to monitor social media in real-time.

CODE

```python
import matplotlib.pyplot as plt
import matplotlib.patches as mpatches

fig, ax = plt.subplots(figsize=(12, 8))
```

Create a diagram using rectangles and arrows

```python
exercise_labels = ['Data Collection', 'Feature Engineering', 'Model
    Training', 'Deployment']
rect_positions_ex = [(0.1, 0.7), (0.1, 0.5), (0.1, 0.3), (0.1,
    0.1)]
for i, (x, y) in enumerate(rect_positions_ex):
rect = mpatches.FancyBboxPatch((x, y), 0.8, 0.15,
    boxstyle="round,pad=0.1", edgecolor='black',
    facecolor='lightblue')
ax.add_patch(rect)
ax.text(x + 0.4, y + 0.075, exercise_labels[i], ha='center',
    va='center', fontsize=12)
```

Add arrows

```python
arrow_positions_ex = [((0.5, 0.675), (0.5, 0.625)),
((0.5, 0.475), (0.5, 0.425)),
((0.5, 0.275), (0.5, 0.225))]
for start, end in arrow_positions_ex:
ax.annotate('', xy=end, xytext=start,
arrowprops=dict(facecolor='black', shrink=0.05, width=2,
    headwidth=8))
ax.set_title('Designing a Social Media Monitoring System',
    fontsize=16, fontweight='bold')
ax.axis('off')
plt.tight_layout()
plt.savefig("/mnt/data/Social_Media_Monitoring_System.png")
plt.show()
```

Made in the USA
Coppell, TX
26 January 2025